WHO BELONGS IN QUEBEC?

WHO BELONGS IN QUEBEC?

Identity Politics in a Changing Society

BY
RAQUEL FLETCHER

Prepared for the press by Kaiya Smith Blackburn
Author photo by Raquel Fletcher
Cover image: Shutterstock
Cover design by Debbie Geltner
Book design by Tika eBooks

Library and Archives Canada Cataloguing in Publication

Title: Who belongs in Quebec? : identity politics in a changing society / by Raquel Fletcher.
Names: Fletcher, Raquel, author.
Identifiers: Canadiana (print) 20190223413 | Canadiana (ebook) 20190223448 | ISBN 9781773900568 (softcover) | ISBN 9781773900575 (HTML) | ISBN 9781773900582 (Kindle) | ISBN 9781773900599 (PDF)
Subjects: LCSH: Identity politics—Québec (Province) | LCSH: Political culture—Québec (Province) | LCSH: Québec (Province)—Race relations—Political aspects. | LCSH: Québec (Province)—Ethnic relations—Political aspects. | LCSH: Minorities—Québec (Province)—Social conditions.
Classification: LCC FC2950.A1 F54 2019 | DDC 305.8009714—dc23

Printed and bound in Canada.

The publisher gratefully acknowledges the support of the Government of Canada through the Canada Council for the Arts and the Canada Book Fund, and of the Government of Quebec through the Société de développement des entreprises culturelles (SODEC).

Linda Leith Publishing
Montreal
www.lindaleith.com

For Grampa

Table of Contents

Introduction

They told us they would send us home if we were caught speaking English. For three days, I made a valiant effort. I had stoically admitted ignorance when the lady at the convenience store did not understand my accent when I asked for stamps. I sucked it up, and told myself I would write letters back home to family anyway and send them when I could. I had courageously eaten the *creton* they served us for breakfast without knowing what it was. And I almost cried with relief when I learned the word for "soap" and could finally ask the resident assistant for some for my dorm. But at the end of those three days, I was defeated.

La Pocatière is a small, picturesque city on the shore of the St. Lawrence, just over an hour north-east of Quebec City—and my new home for a five-week French immersion program. I had never seen such a luscious green landscape nor tasted strawberries so sweet. And I had never been so frustrated. I was a 19-year-old prairie girl away from home for the first time, unable to speak with my family for longer than twenty minutes a week (as per the immersion rules), and I knew so little French that I couldn't speak much with anyone else. A fellow student from Saskatchewan I'd bonded with proposed a cheat day. She suggested we find a local bar somewhere off campus where none of the professors would hear us speak English.

That's where we met Albert. We had to make him write his name down on a napkin before we understood—the way he pronounced it, without the "t" at the end, made *Albert* sound so foreign to me. It was in that bar, over one-too-many pints of Quebec-brewed blonde beer that I learned this province—which refers to itself as a nation—had more to teach me than just French as a second language. For the next two hours, we discussed everything from politics, to travel, to Canadian identity in our limited French and Albert's equally limited English. Out of necessity, we also turned to pantomime and rough sketches on bar napkins. He even wrote us a list of all the main Québécois swear words—the most important French vocabulary we should learn, he told us.

I had applied to this program because I wanted to be bilingual. This was a must, because I wanted to become a political journalist. I hadn't expected to fall in love with this language, this culture, this people. I found a people as curious about the world as I was, willing to spend hours miming out words to help me learn French, teach me new expressions, and share their culture with open arms.

Eight years later, I moved to Quebec permanently, having accepted a job as the National Assembly correspondent for Global News. I knew that reporting in Quebec would be one of the biggest challenges of my career, especially as an anglophone journalist interpreting what happens here for the rest of the country. How, for instance, do you explain that this "staunchly secular" society—as a former assistant news director once described it—also demands that the Ministry of Culture and Communications pour millions of dollars into the preservation of its old churches?

Quebec is a society full of inconsistencies. While it's arguably the most feminist and progressive province in Canada,[1] it's also the only jurisdiction in North America to limit civil liberties by banning religious symbols.[2] It's increasingly modern, global, diverse, and multicultural, particularly in Montreal—and yet, some nationalists defend what could be characterized as anti-immigration policies in the name of protecting the French language. In this respect, the political context in Quebec is indeed distinct from that of the rest of Canada.

That's what makes the story of Quebec so gripping and so difficult to report. There are journalists—particularly journalists who aren't reporting from Quebec—who sometimes miss important nuances, especially when it comes to the religious symbols debate. Getting this issue right is part of the impetus for this book.

In recent years, since the 2017 Quebec City mosque shooting and the political debates leading up to the new Coalition Avenir Québec (CAQ) government's partial ban on religious symbols, Bill 21, many commentators and politicians, in the rest of Canada especially, have asked: "Are Quebecers racist? Islamophobic?" You may have asked yourself the same question.

There must, after all, be some undercurrent of intolerance that led 28-year-old Alexandre Bissonnette to walk into a mosque

---

[1] Four out of the five top cities ranked by the Canadian Centre for Policy Alternatives (CCPA) in 2019 as the best cities for women to live are in Quebec. The CCPA points out that Quebec cities have some of the smallest wage gaps "in part because of progressive family policies that help women balance work and family life, including low-fee child care." Katherine Scott, "The Best and Worst Places to be a Woman in Canada," Behind the Numbers, accessed November 11, 2019, https://bit.ly/2KbB5rn.

[2] Bill 21, passed in June 2019, bans some public employees considered to be in "authority positions"—i.e., judges, Crown prosecutors, police officers, prison guards, and teachers—from wearing religious symbols while at work. The law grants a grandfather clause to employees who had already been hired as long as they stay in their current function.

and fire off nearly fifty rounds of ammunition, killing six people and wounding nineteen others. Bissonnette pleaded guilty and was sentenced to life in prison with no chance of parole for forty years. In a police interrogation video, Bissonnette admits he targeted the mosque because he believed some of the worshipers were Islamist terrorists.

Despite this, Quebec Premier François Legault still told a room full of journalists that he didn't believe Islamophobia existed in Quebec. This unequivocal statement was met with surprise and disbelief, particularly from Muslim groups across the country who called for him to take back his comment.

In another incident that garnered national headlines, a small group of Quebecers succeeded in blocking a private land sale in their community, thus preventing plans for a Muslim cemetery from going ahead—and this in spite of the fact that the bodies of five of the six victims of the mosque attack had to be repatriated to the countries of their birth because there was nowhere here to bury them.

Many have criticized the fact that in Quebec's quest to establish official secularism in the province, some religious symbols—such as crosses and crucifixes—are tolerated, even when they appear prominently, such as on the provincial flag or in public institutions, while others—hijabs and turbans, for instance—are viewed as ostentatious, oppressive or unacceptable.

Following the election of American President Donald Trump, Quebec has also seen the emergence of alt-right groups alongside an emboldened populist and anti-immigration sentiment. François Legault has even been described as the Trump of Quebec.[3] During the 2018 Quebec election campaign, when identity, immigration, and nationalism were major political issues, the Que-

[3] Mathieu Dion, "#assnat/ François Legault, le Donald Trump du Québec?" *Radio-Canada*, November 11, 2016, https://bit.ly/2sOn9gS.

bec Liberal Party accused the CAQ of "intolerance," "racism," and "ethnic nationalism."

But this is not the full story.

When I moved here in 2016, it was clear that the accommodation of cultural diversity had become a necessary new reality for Quebec. As in the rest of the country, it is a reality that is sometimes embraced and at other times meets with hostility. At one time, Quebec was much more homogenous than it is today—to be Québécois meant being white, francophone, Roman Catholic, and even in some cases, working class. Now Quebecers have to contend with the fact that a common national identity will be more and more difficult to define—if such a thing as a "Quebec identity" can still exist in an ever-evolving and increasingly global society.

When the CAQ came into power with a sweeping majority, it quickly introduced Bill 21 and another controversial bill to reform Quebec's immigration system; this was to limit the number of immigrants allowed into the province and impose a values test. Quebec has been severely criticized for these measures in English-language media across the country, but the Premier has been unapologetic about his decisions, saying it's his job to represent what Quebecers want, not to justify them to the rest of Canada.

Heading into the second quarter of the twenty-first century, however, Quebecers will have to justify their decisions to *themselves*. During public hearings for Bill 21, people speaking in favour of the bill and those speaking against it often seemed to be talking past one another. Can those supporting diversity and those supporting the protection of traditional Quebec culture agree on a common national project? They might have to. Even as Quebec City "trash radio" hosts with large, loyal followings continue to make openly discriminatory comments on air, more and more Quebecers are fighting to carve out space for minority views in the public discourse. Quebecers are wrestling with the same question: "Who is allowed to belong here?"

Chapter 1
Blowing on the Embers of Intolerance

The bar was packed, and everyone was in good spirits when I arrived at Iknox, a small pub full of flat-screen TVs on Quebec City's Grande Allée, for an exclusive 2016 US presidential election viewing party for members of the press tribune, as well as politicians and their staff from the National Assembly. I had been to Iknox once before for a beer and knew about their delicious European hot-dogs. I ordered one immediately. The place was fast filling up.

Members of the various Quebec political parties and journalists rarely agreed on anything, except when it came to who should be the next president of the United States, but this was an unusually cohesive group—united in its jubilance as the first results came in. We were impatient to put the past two years of nearly incomprehensible campaign madness behind us, and we knew we were about to bear witness to history, as the first woman made it to the Oval Office.

There were two large cardboard cutouts of the candidates at the entrance to the bar. A colleague and I posed smiling on either side of a beaming Hillary Clinton, whom we were sure would become the first woman president. Canadians, in general, almost overwhelmingly supported Clinton for president. An Ipsos poll conducted on behalf of Global News on November 6, 2016 found 76 percent of Canadians thought Clinton was the best choice for the United States, and 82 percent thought she would be better for Canada.[4] A Mainstreet poll found that 68 percent of Canadians say they would have voted for Clinton and 17 percent for Trump.[5]

We would indeed witness history, but it wasn't at all what we expected. By midnight, the once jovial party had turned somber. No one spoke. We barely moved, not even to re-fill our drinks. We downed them quietly and then stared for a long time into the bottom of our glasses before putting them back on the table. The bar that had been packed was now less than half full. I could feel a ball of anxiety in the pit of my stomach. My colleagues all had the same incredulous expression on their faces. There was still time for the results to turn around, but somehow we knew that wasn't going to happen.

"Should we go?" I asked.

They nodded.

Once outside, I could feel a heaviness on my chest: why was I so affected by the results of another country's presidential election?

Any political journalist anywhere could have told you that night in November was the beginning of drastic change. That Christmas, in my annual letter to friends and family, I wrote, "I have a lot of apprehension for 2017 .... There is constant concern that the words we write and the words we say could incite violence. Although I'm worried about this, right now is also one of the most exciting and important times to be a journalist. And I

---

[4] From a Global News Ipsos poll: Leslie Young, "Canadians rooting for Hillary Clinton to become president: poll" Global News, November 6, 2016, https://globalnews.ca/news/3047708/canadians-rooting-for-hillary-clinton-to-become-president-poll/.

[5] From a Mainstreet/Postmedia poll released November 8, 2016.

feel like I'm in the best position to make a difference."

When I wrote that, I had no way of knowing that a gunman would walk into a mosque only a month later with an assault rifle and a 9mm handgun, open-firing during evening prayers. We later learned that Prime Minister Justin Trudeau's reaction to Trump's Muslim travel ban had, in part, pushed the shooter over the edge. Was Trump's presidency emboldening bigots and racists? What sinister undercurrent was taking hold of the political and social climate south and now north of the border?

A group of Ontario Tech University professors summed it up in the international Journal of Hate Studies: "Following Trump's win, posters plastered on telephone poles in Canadian cities invited 'white people' to visit alt-right websites. Neo-Nazis spray painted swastikas on a mosque, a synagogue and a church with a black pastor. Online, a reactionary white supremacist subculture violated hate speech laws with impunity while stereotyping and demonizing non-white people. Most strikingly, in January 2017, Canada witnessed its most deadly homegrown terrorist incident: Alexandre Bissonnette, a right-wing extremist and Trump supporter, murdered six men at the Islamic cultural centre of Quebec City."[6]

We learned that fake news stories shared on Facebook and other social media networks had influenced the US election's outcome.[7] An emerging alt-right movement saw people openly acknowledge they were white supremacists and publicly declare their anti-immigration and pro-Nazi views.[8] Less than a year after the infamous Charlottesville riots in Virginia, which had left one

[6] Barbara Perry et. al., "The Dangers of Porous Borders," *Journal of Hate Studies*, 14, no. 1 (2019): 53, accessed November 11, 2019, http://doi.org/10.33972/jhs.124.

[7] Danielle Kurtzleben, "Did Fake News on Facebook Help Elect Trump? Here's What We Know," *NPR*, April 11, 2018, https://n.pr/2KaR9JM.

[8] Katie Dangerfield. "White Nationalist Groups on the Rise, Planning More Rallies," *Global News*, August 15, 2017, https://bit.ly/2Kqqvgj.

person dead and injured dozens of others, the Montreal *Gazette* revealed in May 2018 that a well-known neo-Nazi recruiter was living and operating in Quebec's biggest city.[9]

During a scrum in the days following the Quebec City mosque attack, Premier Philippe Couillard deplored how it had become cool to brag about being racist.[10] Identity politics was nothing new in Quebec—the many sides of the ongoing debate about Quebec secularism and a potential ban on religious symbols had created a firestorm of headlines over the years. But was it now coming to a boiling point? Couillard wanted Quebec politicians to tone down the rhetoric, and he made a plea for collaboration from all parties in the National Assembly.

In *Protecting Multiculturalism*, political scientist John McCoy analyzes the tensions surrounding issues of diversity and immigration in Canadian culture and attempts to identify several of its contributing factors. He describes the concept of "xenoracism" as targeting people "who are perceived as foreigners—most especially Muslims." "Xenoracism is intertwined with the seemingly endless global War on Terror," he writes. "The fear of 'Islamic terrorism' that the War on Terror has generated has helped to stimulate public concerns over visible diversity and immigration in Western societies."[11] And this is undermining support for Canada's long-established multiculturalism policy. However, in Quebec, where multiculturalism was never embraced with the same warmth as in English Canada because it adheres "to a more ethni-

---

[9] John Milton et. al., "Exclusive: Major Neo-Nazi Figure Recruiting in Montreal," *The Gazette*, Montreal, May 21, 2018, https://bit.ly/2rAVDD9

[10] In a media scrum on January 31, 2017, with anglophone National Assembly reporters, Couillard said, "It's okay to say, 'I'm a racist.' We've heard that. 'I can say it now. I'm proud of that.' How can someone be proud of that? How come nobody reacts when someone says that?"

[11] John S. McCoy, *Protecting Multiculturalism: Muslims, Security, and Integration in Canada* (Montreal: McGill-Queen's University Press, 2018), 3.

cally rooted vision of national identity,"[12] there are other factors at play. McCoy explains that, "There was concern among nationalists that immigrants were increasingly being integrated into the Anglo minority in Quebec, a trend that was viewed as potentially detrimental to Québécois culture."[13] In other cases, even French-speaking immigrant populations are overlooked or ignored by Quebec's francophone majority, as Cheik Tidiane Ndiaye, an immigrant from Senegal writes. In Quebec City, where he lives, he says, "Visible minorities are most often invisible."[14]

This idea of invisibility is echoed by sociologist Diahara Traoré, who writes that in Quebec, "we don't see" Muslim women from West African countries. "Since the attacks on September 11, 2001, with more and more preponderant scientific research and discussion about Muslims in Western societies," she explains, "the silence of Muslim women from Sub-Saharan Africa is burdensome."[15]

Quebec nationalism, coupled with "the hyperbole of a growing anti-Islamic social movement—a movement that is present, growing and increasingly militant in Canada," as McCoy writes, could be what's at the root of an ongoing debate in Quebec about lowering the number of immigrants the province accepts. The CAQ, elected in October 2018 campaigned on a policy to reduce immigration levels by 10,000 (or 20 percent of current levels),[16]

---

[12] McCoy, *Protecting Multiculturalism*, 105.

[13] McCoy, *Protecting Multiculturalism*, 103.

[14] Cheik Tidiane Ndiaye and Webster, "Québec, 29 Janvier 2017: Je me souviens," in *11 brefs essais contre le racisme pour une lutte systémique*, ed. Christian Nadeau (Montréal : Les éditions Somme toute, 2019), 24.

[15] Diahara Traoré, *Des musulmanes ouest-africaines au Québec: Entre subversion et conformité* (Montréal: Les Presses de l'Université de Montréal, 2019), 5.

[16] Once elected, the CAQ government modified its rhetoric slightly, saying this would be a temporary reduction while it brought in reforms to Quebec's immigration legislation. It also said that it would return to earlier immigration levels by the end of its first mandate.

without fully explaining how it arrived at that number. The party argued that temporarily accepting fewer immigrants would mean more resources available for each newcomer. "*En prendre moins, mais en prendre soin*"—"Take fewer, but take care of them"—became a party slogan. The CAQ had also made election promises to dedicate many of these resources to French-language classes, which it would make mandatory for non-francophone immigrants.

The Liberal Premier Philippe Couillard countered that lowering the number of immigrants when Quebec had a labour shortage was simply bad public policy—and he accused the CAQ of trying to profit from a growing populist movement south of the border. In one memorable Question Period in the National Assembly, Couillard's response to CAQ leader François Legault was quick and immediate: "I'm very afraid, Mr. Speaker, that the [CAQ] is blowing on the embers of intolerance, as it has done in the past." [17]

Couillard has been mocked for his erudite mastery of the French language. He once fired back at a journalist's question he disdained, with a quote from a French translation from Shakespeare's *The Merchant of Venice*, saying: "What do you want, a pound of flesh, a little blood?" This time, though, journalists seized upon Couillard's retort, which was widely reported.

Couillard himself would repeat his comments about blowing on the embers of intolerance several times as the Liberals tried to paint the CAQ as not only anti-immigration, but also anti-immigrant. On May 28, 2018, the Quebec Liberal Party tweeted a new quote from the Premier. "Blowing on the embers of intolerance is not [only] talking about immigration levels." Couillard now said, "It presents a foreigner as someone who must be excluded."

[17] All translations are my own. Louis Gagné, "Immigration: Couillard accuse Legault de 'souffler sur les braises de l'intolérance,'" *Le Journal de Québec*, March 9, 2016, https://bit.ly/350QLWr.

The inflammatory comments and prejudiced policies that have dominated American politics since the 2016 election cannot easily be dismissed as a foreign problem. Quebec has its own problems—religious symbols worn in the public sector, the growing number of asylum seekers crossing into Canada at the US-Quebec border, and the challenge of defining a national Quebec identity, to name just a few—and they are serious and divisive. The CAQ has already tried to address some of these controversial issues and has been rewarded with great acclaim as well as a swift backlash.

The CAQ has also been criticized for its view that neither systemic racism nor Islamophobia exist in Quebec. When the Liberal government proposed to hold public consultations on systemic racism, the CAQ and the Parti Québécois opposition argued this was the equivalent of putting Quebecers "on trial." After the CAQ won a Quebec City by-election in a traditional Liberal stronghold a year before the general provincial election, Couillard decided to cancel the consultations, fearing the controversy surrounding them might lead to defeat. The writer and activist Webster describes his frustration over this decision:

> It's a very ethnocentric vision of Quebec and its demography. I find this attitude so condescending, each time someone says, 'There's no racism here,' 'It's worse in other places,' or 'You don't understand, it's not really that.' As if our opinion didn't count; as if...what minorities experience or think doesn't have the same value as people in the majority.[18]

Will the new government be able to find solutions for the issues that divide us in Quebec *without* blowing on the embers of intolerance that risk igniting the biggest racial and class conflicts

---

[18] Ndiaye, "Québec, 29 Janvier 2017: Je me souviens," 24.

of our time? Those embers, periodically stoked, have been burning for a long time. In the next chapter, I look at how we got here. There's a long history of language and secularism debates in Quebec, filled with important nuances that need to be explored.

Chapter 2
Pastagate, the English-Language Debate, and the Separation of Church and State

One of the first stories I covered as a journalist after moving to Quebec was a language story. Quebec's French-language watchdog had taken issue with the name of a new diner in Quebec City's Limoilou neighbourhood, Resto La Mama Grilled Cheese. Grilled cheese sandwiches, the francophone owners told me, were as québécois as poutine. The fact that the name was too English for the Office québécois de la langue française (OQLF) had them scratching their heads. After all, they said, restaurants in other provinces sold poutine without calling it "fries with gravy and cheese curds." Not to mention the several other food words that Quebecers have borrowed from English: un toast, steak frites, hot dog steamé, and so on. "I could call it '*sandwich de fromage fondu*,'" one of the owners explained, "but then nobody would know what I was selling."

But La Mama Grilled Cheese was possibly in contravention of Bill 101, also known as the Charter of the French Language, which became law in 1977 under Parti Québécois Premier René Lévesque. Defining French as the official language of Quebec, Bill 101 laid out strict rules for education and advertising, stipulating that corporate signage appear first in French, with any English signage underneath in smaller lettering.

Over the decades, Bill 101 has been in many ways successful in promoting and protecting French in Quebec. According to the last census, in 2016, 94.5 percent of people in Quebec were able to speak French (up from 92.5 percent in 1981),[19] thanks in large part to the fact that 89 percent of immigrant children now go to French schools, compared to 15 percent in 1975.[20] For many Quebecers, the fear that French is disappearing in Quebec has diminished.[21] Policing the names of restaurants and menu items is increasingly regarded as not only unnecessary, but also frankly embarrassing at times.

In 2013, for example, Quebec made international headlines when the OQLF decided that an Italian restaurant in Montreal should not use the word "pasta" on its menu. For some people, "Pastagate" —as the controversy was dubbed—proved that the province could become fanatical in the name of protecting its language and culture. And by doing so, it stood the risk of insulating itself from the rest of the world.

As a newcomer to the province, and a *francophile*, I didn't know where to stand on this issue. The daughter of a business owner, I could sympathize with the frustration of young restaurateurs

---

[19] Lachapelle, R. and Lepage, J.F., (2010). *Languages in Canada: 2006 Census. New Canadian Perspectives*. Canadian Heritage.

[20] Robert Calderisi, *Quebec in a Global Light: Reaching for the Common Ground* (Toronto: University of Toronto Press, 2019), 41.

[21] For example, in 2018, according to a report published by the OLQF, 40 percent of francophones in Greater Montreal between 18 and 34 said they were indifferent to being offered a service in another language other than French, which the language watchdog highlighted for being a significant increase from 23 percent in 2012. See OQLF, "Rapport sur l'évolution de la situation linguistique au Québec" (Quebec City, 2018), https://bit.ly/2p8KOax.

who had risked their savings and then been told to purchase new signage and come up with a whole new marketing plan for something as innocuous and harmless as "*un grilled-cheese*" or a plate of pasta.

On the other hand, the need to protect the French language had been drilled into me ever since I enrolled in the French as a Second Language program at the University of Regina when I was nineteen. My professors were active members of a small, fiercely proud minority-language community. Many of them had been battling for the official status of French on the prairies, afraid that without legal protection, the language could soon disappear. They insisted their students remove all anglicisms (or *calques*) from their vocabulary.

Don't say "*bon matin*," they told us, for that's a direct translation of "good morning." Say "*bonjour*," instead. Don't say that you want to travel "à travers le monde" (a direct translation of "around the world"); say "*dans tous les pays du monde*." And so on and so forth. My Fransaskois professors might have had conniptions if they'd heard the way Quebecers littered their speech with English words and expressions. I could visualize the steam coming out of their ears every time one of my new neighbours said something like, "*J'ai callé un pizz*" —I called for a pizza.

Quebecers often adapt English words into French by chopping off all but the first syllable. For instance, a *mush* is a mushroom. A *snow* is a snowboard. Likewise, a *skate* is a skateboard. They also modify the meaning of some English words: if someone makes a reference to their *jogging*, they're talking about their sweatpants, and their *running* is a reference to their running shoes. There are perfectly fine French words for all of these *calques*, but many Quebecers, I soon understood, felt the co-option of English into everyday speech gave their language (and culture) vitality, even worldliness. Not to mention, modern economic progress requires a certain openness to English and other languages and cultures. Quebec was evolving with the times and many questioned if the OQLF was out of date. [22]

When it comes to language issues in Quebec, politicians must straddle a fine line. In his vision for the future of Quebec, the millionaire businessman-turned leader of the Coalition Avenir Québec, François Legault, sees an "innovation valley." In a 2013 book, he describes his plan to model a section of Quebec alongside the St. Lawrence River after California's Silicon Valley.[23] He would like to see the universities in Montreal and Quebec City bolstered in order to foster innovation, research, and design, thereby attracting investment and international talent. The goal of which would be to create high-paying and lucrative jobs in the IT and start-up sectors. While Legault's political opponents have accused him of promoting nationalist values and even a far-right anti-immigrant agenda,[24] he admits that immigration plays a key role in his plan for a St. Lawrence innovation and technology hub. Attracting the world's top tech talent to California, he points out, has meant that 50 percent or more of the people who live and work in Silicon Valley speak a language other than English at home. Now that he had become premier, one can assume that—if he were to see his plan through—in a few decades 50 percent or more of Quebecers living along the St. Lawrence River between Montreal and Quebec City might be expected to speak a language other than French at home.

This said, however, Legault has repeated that it's also impor-

[22] Alison Hanes, "As language tension in Quebec ebbs, what is OQLF to do?" *The Gazette*, Montreal, May 24, 2018, https://bit.ly/2qNvDDV.

[23] François Legault, *Cap sur un Québec gagnant : le projet Saint-Laurent*, Montréal: Les Éditions du Boréal, 1998.

[24] Raquel Fletcher, "Quebec Liberals won't apologize for accusing CAQ of 'ethnic-based nationalism,'" *Global News*, March 15, 2018, https://bit.ly/2qGdmsg.

tant that French not only remain Quebec's *lingua franca* in years to come, but also the majority language in the province.[25] It was in June 2019 that his government passed the bill that would impose mandatory French language classes for new immigrants, followed by a French language exam after three years in the province. Regardless of his or her employment status, if the newcomer is unable to pass the exam, he or she will be refused a selection certificate needed to apply to the federal government for permanent resident status. Opposition parties criticized the government, saying this will only aggravate Quebec's already pronounced labour shortage.

During the 2018 fall election campaign, the PQ—the party responsible for bringing in Quebec's current language laws when it was in government in 1977—put forward a different proposal: that all immigrants be required to speak French before they arrive in Quebec. This was supposed to help counter the decline of French in the province (Based on numbers from the last census, Statistics Canada projects the number of native French-speakers would decline from 77 percent of the population in 2016 to 70 percent by 2036.)[26] The PQ's then leader, Jean-François Lisée, was particularly concerned about French in Montreal, where the number of French-speakers could dip below 50 percent.[27] Even if the vast majority of Quebecers are able to speak French, Lisée argued, the decline in the number of francophones was cause for alarm. He said the true test of the vibrancy of the language and culture is the number of Quebec families who speak French at home.

[25] The Canadian Press, "CAQ says it would expel immigrants who fail to learn French in 3 years," *Global News*, September 7, 2018, https://bit.ly/36TGUDs.

[26] Statistics Canada language projections report (Houle and Corbeil, 2017), cat. No. 89-657-X2017001, reference scenario in Table 3.2 (this is based on 2011 NHS data).

[27] Calderisi, *Quebec in a Global Light*, 32.

"More non-francophones in Quebec speaking French is a marvelous thing, but there is a difference between people who speak French as a second language and people who live in French," he explained. This argument upset Kathleen Weil, then Liberal Minister of Immigration. She said differentiating between Quebecers who spoke French as their mother tongue and Quebecers who spoke French as a second language was dangerous. "This is one of those debates that really does more than irritate me, but worries me, when people put a focus on the language you speak at home," she said. She pointed out that the same Statistics Canada census also found that Quebecers were becoming more and more multilingual, speaking more than 150 different languages at home.[28] Montreal was the city with the most trilingual people in Canada, by far: 21 percent of Montrealers are able to carry on a conversation in three languages compared to only 11 percent in Toronto[29] and that, Weil said, was something to be proud of.

A few days after receiving the original letter from the OQLF (and after a lot of media coverage), *La Mama Grilled Cheese* was told it could keep its signage. Was it a move by the language police to avoid another Pastagate? Maybe, but it was clear that Quebec is at a crossroads. I sometimes think of it as a second Quiet Revolution. Does the province want to become a major economic player on the international stage, with a diversified market that invests in innovation and attracts talent from all over the world? Or does it feel threatened by that very prospect?

Will opening its doors to the world at large inevitably lead to the loss of the French majority, or even of the French language? Protecting French while growing the Quebec economy seems like

[28] Statistics Canada data table Cat. No. 98-400-X2016070.

[29] Guiseppe Valiente (The Canadian Press), "New census numbers show Montreal to be Canada's most trilingual city," *Global News*, December 30, 2017, https://bit.ly/2O1vwg5.

a balancing act for current politicians, but is there another choice? Can Quebec have its cake and eat it too? Could Quebec become a major international cultural hub? Could it be the multi-franco-cultural equivalent to the multicultural mosaic that has become so integral to English Canada's identity?[30] Could cultural communities from French-speaking countries around the world—Europe, Africa, and Asia—be represented in Quebec cities and towns? Might Montreal become the epicentre of francophone culture in a modern cosmopolitan city?

Francophone Leaders Eager to Debate in English

Unexpectedly, it was the PQ leader who was the first to announce that he intended to participate in an English-language leaders' debate organized by a consortium of Quebec English media, including Global News, CTV, CJAD 800, and *The Gazette*. Without even waiting to be asked the question, Jean-François Lisée told English reporters at the National Assembly that he was looking forward to it:

---

[30] There has been strong criticism of multiculturalism in Quebec ever since it was adopted as official federal policy in 1971. In a *Journal de Québec* blog post, Antoine Robitaille writes, "Since the 1970's, many Quebecers have denounced what they considered a ruse from Trudeau *père* to undermine the thesis of 'two founding peoples.'" Robitaille quotes author Neil Bissoondath, who wrote in his 1994 book *Selling Illusions* that he feared multiculturalism would lead to "cultural apartheid." Robitaille goes on to cite the 2007 Bouchard-Taylor Report that coined the term "interculturalism." He explains that Bouchard and Taylor "preferred Quebec's interculturalism to Canadian multiculturalism because it promotes—at least in theory a 'culture of convergence.' In other words, we can very well be in favour of diversity, but there are several ways to conceive of it and organize it." Antoine Robitaille, "'Pure laine,' moi ? Réplique à un tweet dégueulasse," *Journal de Montréal*, August 22, 2018, https://bit.ly/2CxzEz7.

> I think there is much to tell the Anglo population of Quebec about how they've been taken for granted by the Liberals and how they've been hurt, as a community and as Quebecers, by the Liberals' policies."

Mr. Couillard, he argued, had much to answer for in French and English, and that was why Lisée was in favour of a leaders' debate in English.

A vibrant, albeit predominantly federalist and Liberal, English-speaking community has always existed in the province. Yet, despite the fact that over 600,000 people speak English as their mother tongue in Quebec, with more identifying it as their primary language in the home,[31] there had never before in the history of Quebec been a televised English debate between the leaders of political parties.

When it was announced that the English debate was going ahead, not everyone was enthusiastic. "Let's admit it," Josée Legault wrote in the *Journal de Montréal*, "the ambition to form a truly distinct nation by its language and culture, while staying inside Canada, is quietly leaving us."[32]

The leaders agreed to participate in a televised English debate, she explains, "as though Quebec were nothing more than a small bilingual inverted Canada .... Since 1974, the only official language in Quebec is French. A respect for this fundamental principle should go without saying for all those who govern or aspire to govern."

TVA commentator Mario Dumont said on air he was "profoundly against" the idea., unveiling what he called "the real reason" for holding the debate in English: that Jean-François Lisée

---

[31] Statistics Canada data table Cat. No. 98-400-X2016345.

[32] Josée Legault, "Une province full bilingue," *Journal de Montréal*, May 3, 2018, https://bit.ly/2CB3McZ.

speaks English very well, better than the others. Dumont swiftly added, "Democracy is not a game!"[33]

Despite concerns from some commentators, the leaders of Quebec's four main political parties eagerly participated in the televised English debate on September 17, 2018.[34] The first subject was education, and Legault's plan to bring in province-wide pre-kindergarten for 4-year-olds soon came under attack by Liberal leader Philippe Couillard, especially as the cost of the program was not included in the CAQ's financial plan.

"By the way, you're a doctor. I'm a chartered accountant. I think I know the numbers better than you," Legault said.

Couillard was ready with a quick comeback: "M. Legault, if my accountant had given me this statement, I would have fired him."

Lisée piped up, addressing a question to "the accountant." "You have promised to cut $700 million in school taxes every year," he said. "You think we can afford that?"

When Lisée pushed further on his rival's plan to lower school taxes, debate moderator Debra Arbec had had enough.

"That is not the topic. That is not the topic," Arbec protested, trying to cut in, but the leaders spoke over her.

"Mr. Lisée. Mr. Lisée. Mr. Lisée. Mr. Legault. Mr. Lisée," she insisted, "That is not the topic."

When she turned to Manon Massé for an answer to the original question, the leader of Québec Solidaire jokingly asked if the topic being discussed was still education. The debate was just getting started—and it was about to get a lot more heated. For the first

---

[33] "Quelle est la 'vraie raison' de la tenue du débat en anglais? " TVA Nouvelles, September 17, 2018, video, https://bit.ly/36XQHZ1.

[34] This 90-minute televised debate, which took place at the Maison Radio-Canada in Montreal, was produced by a consortium of English-language media outlets, including CBC, CTV News, Global News, City, CJAD 800 and *The Gazette*.

time in a long time, sovereignty was not one of the main points of contention during a Quebec election campaign. Moreover, the two traditionally dominant political parties—the Liberals (a party created in 1867) and the PQ (which was founded in 1968)—had now given way to a four-party system, which included the CAQ (created in 2011) and Québec Solidaire (created in 2006). Instead of sovereignty, the hot-button issues were education, health care, the economy, and the particularly explosive topic of immigration. Arbec and co-moderator Mutsumi Takahashi had to interrupt more than once to get the debate back under control.

Couillard drilled Legault because he said the CAQ leader refused to acknowledge Quebec's labour shortage as a major problem, and one that he insisted immigration could help solve. The Liberal leader went further, saying Legault's proposed values and linguistic tests were proof the CAQ wants to "get rid of immigrants" by removing people who fail the tests. "I want them to stay here," Couillard said. "I want immigrants who are here to partake in the growth that we have. We need newcomers to match our needs."

Legault fired back, claiming that many immigrants leave Quebec soon after they arrive. "We have to change the way we choose new immigrants," he argued. "How come we lose 26 percent of immigrants? If immigration is the solution (to the labour shortage) why do we lose 26 percent? Can you admit that this is a failure of your government?"[35]

"Not at all," Couillard replied. "M. Legault is trying to find a way to decrease immigrants, whatever his problem is with immigrants, we don't know .... I asked him about a family the other

[35] A 2016 Fraser Institute report found that Quebec lost almost 600,000 residents to other provinces between 1971 and 2015, the only Canadian province to have suffered an annual net loss. Jason Clemens *et al.*, "Interprovincial Migration in Canada: Quebeckers Vote With Their Feet," last modified June 28, 2016, https://bit.ly/2O0fgfo.

day—and what they would do if the father flunked his exam—and he couldn't answer." Then, turning directly to Legault, he said, "I guess you'll just drop them at the Macdonald-Cartier Bridge in Gatineau and say, 'Get rid of these people.'"

"This is so nonsensical," Lisée said, agreeing with Couillard. "Don't you know when they pass those [federal] tests to become citizens, if they fail, they can stay in Quebec as landed immigrants? You would have the federal government expel them. That's appalling."

The three men went head-to-head once again, with the moderators interrupting several times to allow Massé to have a say. "We [Québec Solidaire] are the only party in the last few years who supports a public inquiry on systemic discrimination. None of them was able to do that," she said, "and we know that systemic discrimination exists in Quebec." She added that only 3 percent of the hires in the public service under the last government were visible minorities. She then proposed implementing quotas, but as soon as she finished speaking, Couillard and Legault were at it again.

"It's distressful to hear you speak about immigration the way you do. Submitting people to testing that is not needed. Threatening … them and their families with expulsion," Couillard argued.

"That's right," Lisée chimed in.

"Incredible," said Legault.

"What is incredible?" Couillard asked.

"What you say. It's unacceptable," Legault replied.

"It's your program, sir," said Lisée.

"You cannot discuss in a calm way about integration. You failed," Legault said, directing his response to Couillard.

"You would be worse," Lisee retorted to Legault. "Asking people to come here and in three years' time, saying 'I may ask

Ottawa to deport you.' That's worse than him! He didn't do enough to integrate; you would scare them away."

The camera panned to a very quiet Massé massaging her temples as her male counterparts argued.

Quebec Secularism

Given the global refugee crisis and the tension surrounding the issue of immigration in the world, Couillard predicted that it would also be the single most important issue of the Quebec election as well.[36] "When people say they [immigrants] are a threat to French language in Quebec … it's nonsense," Couillard said during the English-language debate. "It's not helping. They have to feel welcomed, [especially] by the political leaders." Couillard was likely referring to the often-heated rhetoric that concerns the issue of immigration, and is also tied to a decades-long debate over Quebec secularism and reasonable religious accommodations.

In 2007, the Jean Charest government dished out approximately $5 million for the now famous Bouchard-Taylor Commission led by Gérard Bouchard, a historian and sociologist from University of Quebec in Chicoutimi, and philosopher Charles Taylor from McGill University. This followed headlines like the Hérouxville "code of conduct": although there were no immigrants in this small hamlet, the town council voted unanimously in 2007 for a code which listed unacceptable cultural practices,

---

[36] Raquel Fletcher, "Immigration the 'ballot box' question in Quebec election, Couillard says," *Global News*, September 10, 2018, https://bit.ly/33ET8O2.

such as stoning and female genital mutilation.[37] Controversy also arose that same year when a YMCA installed frosted windows after an ultra-Orthodox Jewish synagogue next door complained they could see girls and women working out in gym clothes.[38]

Among the recommendations in their final report, Bouchard and Taylor suggested that public employees in positions of coercive authority, like judges, Crown prosecutors, police officers, prison guards, and the speaker of the National Assembly be barred from wearing religious signs, such as crosses, hijabs, kippahs, or turbans. After hearing testimony from a wide range of Quebecers and interviewing numerous experts, the Commission recommended that public employees without such power, like teachers, students, public servants, health professionals, and all others be allowed to wear religious signs at work and school.

The Commission also made other recommendations to foster harmony in a multicultural society, what Quebec refers to as the *vivre-ensemble* (literally "living together"): medical patients should not be allowed to choose care providers based on gender, for example; private and public employers should adopt paid leave for religious holidays; and the large crucifix hanging over the speaker's chair in the National Assembly should be relocated elsewhere in the Quebec parliament.

Since the publication of the Commission's report, religious accommodations and state neutrality have been a key issue in four general elections, resulting in one minority and three majority governments. Though often referred to as the Bouchard-Taylor

---

[37] This code of conduct made international news, including at Fox News and the BBC. It's one of the defining examples of the reasonable accommodations debate going on at that time in Quebec. Graeme Hamilton. "The Hérouxville Code." National Post. December 30, 2007, http://www.nationalpost.com/h%C3%A9rouxville+code/206887/story.html.

[38] "Montreal YMCA drops tinted windows after members protest." *CBC News*. March 19, 2007, https://bit.ly/2s45JwA.

consensus, or the Bouchard-Taylor *compromise*, the attempts to bring in legislation based on those recommendations have nevertheless caused nothing but division. "We haven't made up our minds in the last fifteen years," the PQ leader Jean-François Lisée told morning news host Laura Casella in November 2016. "And that's the worst possible scenario. We have to make up our minds, make a decision, and move on."[39]

No political party agreed with the recommendations on the whole: some believed they went too far, while others wanted the province to go farther still. Then, shortly after the Quebec City mosque shooting, Charles Taylor pulled his support for his own report, publishing an open letter in *La Presse+*, an online newspaper, explaining why he changed his mind about banning religious symbols for government employees in positions of authority.[40] "It's principally the evolution of the context that has made me change my opinion," he wrote, adding that continuing to hammer on the point of religious symbols will only act to further "stigmatize minorities."

Quebec had already rejected the so-called Charter of Values, introduced in 2013 by Bernard Drainville, then the Parti Québécois Democratic Institutions Minister and now a popular radio personality. The charter would have seen all public employees, not just those in so-called authority positions, lose their jobs for wearing any type of religious symbol. It turned out to be a highly divisive piece of legislation and helped to topple the PQ minority government in 2014.

In the wake of the mosque shooting, the political context was that of a community deeply divided over the issue of immigra-

---

[39] "Jean-François Lisée Talks Quebec Identity," *Global News*, November 25, 2016, https://bit.ly/33F44eC.

[40] Charles Taylor, "Opinion: Neutralité de l'état: le temps de la reconciliation," *La Presse+*, February 14, 2017, https://bit.ly/2p7bCYA.

tion, and Charles Taylor was asking for an end to the debate in Quebec for good. "We have experienced a horrible attack, but it was followed by a true explosion of solidarity and mutual recognition between Quebecers of all origins," Taylor wrote. "We are starting to overcome the divisions, to fill in the pitfalls, and to sew up the tears in our social fabric .... Let's not re-open the wounds. Let's leave a place for the time for reconciliation."

The CAQ government elected in October 2018 with a sweeping majority, however, claimed that secularism legislation was needed before Quebec could put an end to this debate. It introduced its own controversial pieces of legislation: the bill to reform Quebec's immigration system and limit the number of immigrants allowed to come into the province, and the secularism bill, which includes a partial religious symbols ban.

Chapter 3
Zero Sum Game: The Challenge of Defining Quebec Identity

When the idea of a leaders' debate in English was floated before the 2014 provincial election, *Journal de Montréal* columnist Mathieu Bock-Côté wrote that he was concerned this would set a negative precedent. "We hear little by little the idea of French Quebec giving way to a bilingual Quebec," he explained, "French is no longer considered the sole official language, nor the common language. It's now one of two. The linguistic legacy of the Quiet Revolution has been denied." [41]

Prominent Quebec journalist Michel C. Auger disagreed with Côté's cynicism. He argued that, unfortunately, some view the long-standing language debate as "a zero sum game." "If there is English anywhere, even a single syllable, that must inevitably mean that French is in decline," he wrote.[42] He also criticized "the reflex to prohibit," which exists in the context of immigration and secularism. For instance, he argued the reflex to ban religious signs "is stronger than that to adopt measures that promote the

[41] Mathieu Bock-Côté, "Un débat des chefs en anglais?" *Journal de Montréal*, March 3, 2014, https://bit.ly/2KbLnb0.

[42] Michel C. Auger, *25 mythes à déboulonner en politique Québécoise* (Montréal : Les Éditions La Presse, 2018).

integration of newcomers of the Muslim faith."

In his book, Auger points out that while Quebec currently welcomes tens of thousands of educated, qualified newcomers each year, it struggles to convince them to stay here. He writes, "The non-recognition of diplomas and foreign work experience is the principal obstacle in this matter. It's just as curious that Quebec selects its foreign immigrants precisely on the basis of credentials and work experience that are not worth much once they arrive here."[43] According to a 2016 Institut du Québec study, immigrants with university degrees are the least successful newcomers to the province, particularly those university graduates who are of the Muslim faith.

Auger says that there are still Quebecers who believe immigration thresholds should be lowered "not for demographic reasons, but because immigrants don't integrate themselves into the francophone majority." The growing visibility of different cultures, particularly Muslim cultures has, for some people who belong to the French-speaking majority, come to signal a threat to Quebec identity, for which a ban on religious symbols is supposed to protect. "But what is the most worrying," he says, "is realizing that what was first presented as a way to establish secularism, has come to be seen in very little time as a defense of Quebec identity, as if Quebec identity hinged on banning Muslim religious signs."[44]

During the 2018 provincial election campaign, Laval University political scientist Thierry Giasson said French in Quebec is not threatened—more than 94 percent of Quebecers speak French. "To say that immigration is a threat to French society is not recognizing the impact that Bill 101 has had on the preservation of French in our society," he said.[45] Like Auger, Giasson points out

---

[43] Auger, *25 Mythes*, 39

[44] Auger *25 Mythes*, 48.

[45] Thierry Giasson, in a *Global News* interview, September 12, 2018.

that Quebec's political parties talk a lot about immigration, but few promise to invest in helping newcomers settle and stay in Quebec. "They're spending left and right on social programs, on tax cuts, on dental care, every one of them," he maintains, "Yet none of [the political parties] except for the Liberals have committed to investing more in immigrant integration." He says this might be deliberate: a way for the Coalition Avenir Québec (CAQ) or Parti Québécois (PQ) to pander to that French-speaking majority, even though their platforms do not propose the best public policy. For instance, the PQ said that it would only accept French-speaking immigrants, arguing this would make accommodation and integration easier, though this proposal ignored the fact that language is not the only reason immigrants choose to stay or leave Quebec. "A quarter to 40 percent of French immigrants from France are leaving," Giasson said, citing both cultural and economic reasons.

In the summer before the 2018 Quebec election—after leaving the Conservative Party to form his own political party—Quebec MP Maxime Bernier set off a debate about the limits of immigration and multiculturalism. Where should Canada draw the line on diversity? he asked in a series of tweets sent on August 12. Further, he stressed that,

> Canada is today one of the countries where people have the most freedom to express their identity. But why should we promote ever more diversity? If anything and everything is Canadian, does being Canadian mean something? Shouldn't we emphasize our cultural traditions, what we have built and have in common, what makes us different from other cultures and societies?

Bernier also tweeted that more diversity would divide Canadians "into little tribes that have less and less in common":

> Having people live among us who reject basic Western values such as freedom, equality, tolerance, and openness doesn't make us strong. People who refuse to integrate into our society and want to live apart in their ghetto don't make our society strong ....

Cultural balkanization, he argued, results in distrust, social conflict, and potentially in violence. It was time, in Bernier's view, to reverse this trend.

The following day, he added that Canada has always been diverse and that this is part of who we are.

> I love this Canada. But there is a difference between recognizing diversity and pushing for ever more of it. Something infinitely diverse has no core identity and ceases to exist.

He seemed to be displaying a more extreme brand of anti-immigrant sentiment that has evolved over time in Quebec politics, and which many people have found offensive. He continued the tweets for several days, but he refused to grant any interviews with mainstream media to explain his comments. Bernier also refused an interview for this book. I would have liked to ask him if he really believed that Canada would cease to exist if it became more diverse. And how much diversity did he consider too much diversity?

Lowering Immigration

Once the CAQ started climbing in the polls in the second half of 2017, the Liberals and the PQ took turns accusing the CAQ of promoting divisive, extreme-right views and questioned two of its established policy ideas in particular. The first was a plan to reduce the number of immigrants accepted in Quebec each year from 50,000 to 40,000, and the second was to make newcomers pass a "Quebec values test." The CAQ released a detailed immigration policy document in May 2018, but didn't provide any examples of questions that would appear on that test. They questions would be determined by an independent body once the party was in power, they said, and would be circumscribed by the Quebec Charter of Human Rights and Freedoms.

One day I took a taxi, and the driver, a recent immigrant from West Africa, was telling me about the challenge he faced getting his veterinarian credentials recognized in Quebec. He was saving up to write an exam that would allow him to practise; he estimated this would cost over $10,000. I asked him what he thought about the proposed values test he might also one day be forced to take. He didn't understand the point of such a test.

"Quebec values?" he asked, "These are universal values." The veterinarian/taxi driver felt that most people understand basic human rights, including equality between men and women. However, he said, the CAQ was insisting that newcomers should have to *demonstrate* that they understand this in order to prove they will be able to integrate into Quebec society. "A part of the population is worried about immigration, and if you don't establish clear rules, then you have major problems," Legault said in November 2016 at a party convention where the CAQ adopted a motion to force all non-francophone immigrants to take French-language classes.

In an interview with the Montreal *Gazette* in March 2018, Liberal Finance Minister Carlos Leitao pushed back against this philosophy. "The kind of nationalism the CAQ proposes is, in my opinion, an ethnic-based nationalism. I'm not afraid of the words. This is what it is. They view the French majority as being under attack from all those foreigners out there," he said. The following month, his colleague, Justice Minister Stéphanie Vallée made a similar accusation in the National Assembly, directing her criticism towards CAQ Immigration critic, Natalie Roy. She said, "Over the past four years, [Roy] and her political party have taken pleasure in whacking minorities, whacking newcomers, with their exclusion tests .... Are Quebec families only white and francophone, according to the CAQ?"

Leitao's comments made headlines and started another battle between the Liberals and the CAQ. *Gazette* columnist Don Macpherson wrote that it was easy to dismiss Leitao's attack on the "ethnic-based nationalism" of the CAQ party as a sign of the Liberal government's desperation at the possibility of electoral defeat. However, Macpherson argued:

> "... the uproar over his reference to ethnic nationalism diverted attention away from the fact that for once, a Quebec politician had acknowledged a serious problem in the province's politics: the poisonous divisiveness of Quebec nationalism.[46]

Macpherson went on to say that, in his opinion, Quebec nationalism categorizes people into good and bad Quebecers. Good Quebecers are francophones, or at least speak French at home. Bad Quebecers are those who speak another language at home, even if they speak French at work and in public. "And, as Leitao said, nationalists see the bad ones as outsiders, and as threats to the language, culture and values of the majority, which must protect itself through the government and the legislature it controls." By

[46] Don Macpherson, "Nationalism divides us into good and bad Quebecers." *The Gazette* (Montreal), March 17, 2018.

putting Quebecers in two separate categories—the native versus the stranger; the *Québécois de souche* (old stock Quebecers) versus newcomers; francophone Quebecers versus anglophone Quebecers—the zero-sum game had begun.

When the Personal Is the Political

Carlos Leitao immigrated to Montreal from Portugal when he was 16 years old. The Liberal Finance Minister, who speaks both French and English, had long been outspoken (in both languages) about any policies that have the potential to divide Quebecers. The issue, for him, was personal. In the National Assembly, he told me in a November 2016 interview, he often had to bite his lip because "sometimes I think I'm going to explode and say something I'm going to regret." What gets him to that point? "The proposition that immigrants are a threat to Quebec, or to Quebec society." [47]

The election of a majority Liberal government in 2014 saw the end of the PQ's Charter of Values, but a debate over immigration continued, particularly when the CAQ began floating its plan to reduce the number of immigrants arbitrarily, according to Leitao, by 20 percent. Lowering immigrant thresholds is a complex subject, but in the current global political climate in 2018, it was sure to become a major election issue. If the CAQ's immigration plan was a deliberate strategy to score political points with populist voters, by the end of 2017, it appeared to be working: the CAQ was leading in all polls. At the same time, the Liberal government's attempt to bring in secularism legislation made international headlines and caused a media firestorm that saw Que-

[47] Raquel Fletcher, "Quebec Finance Minister Carlos Leitao reflects on life as a young immigrant in the province," *Global News*, November 28, 2016, https://bit.ly/36g1oF8.

bec once again accused of religious discrimination.

Who's Allowed to Ride the Bus?

My francophone brother-in-law was not about to let the passenger get away with not saying anything as he exited the city bus. "It's been a real pleasure, eh?" he said sarcastically in his abrupt style, just loud enough to get the man's attention, but not so obnoxious that the man would take offence. In fact, he looked more startled than anything.. "Uh yeah, thank you," he stammered. It was a typical Sunday morning at my mother-in-law's house for one of our regular family breakfasts, and my brother-in-law was shooting the breeze about his job. He took pride in his work as an RTC (Réseau de transport de la Capitale) bus driver in Quebec City, and passengers who didn't say "hello" when they got on or "thank you" when they got off really ground his gears.

I'd noticed that bus drivers in Quebec's capital were remarkably friendly, and now I understood why. It was part of the bus culture. As we sat around the table devouring our bacon and eggs, as well as my mother-in-law's famous meat pâté, I anxiously wondered if I'd ever been so caught up in my own world that I'd gotten off a bus without acknowledging the driver. From then on, I decided I would always make a point of greeting my driver with a friendly smile and thanking him or her once I reached my destination. My brother-in-law had a point. After all, he was a person offering a service to another person. In my case, it was a big service, as I hate driving. Taking the RTC allows me to read the morning news, while someone else deals with the stress of early morning traffic. It was an important reminder that, even in our increasingly erratic contemporary world, we still live in a world of daily human interaction.

That's why it was so jarring—and for many regular riders like me, even a little unnerving to see bus drivers, in the fall of 2017, drawn into the centre of a messy political battle on identity. For many Quebec families like my in-laws, the discussion of politics never went beyond the breakfast table. Once Sunday brunch was over, we all packed up our opinions and went back to our daily lives. However, for a few confusing weeks that autumn in 2017, it seemed that bus drivers, those friendly municipal employees that greeted people on and off public transport, were going to be forced to play a crucial role in determining which Quebecers had the right to receive that public service based on his or her religious practices. Unions questioned if bus drivers would have to become Quebec's identity police.[48] Could they—would they—really kick someone off the bus for wearing a religious headscarf? And what kind of repercussions could they face if they were dragged into court on a constitutional charge?

Let's back up.

How did Quebec's religious accommodations debate lead the government to legislate who could and couldn't ride the bus? In 2015, in an attempt to put an end to the accommodation debate, as well as finally determine when it was appropriate to wear religious symbols in public, the governing Liberals introduced Bill 62: An Act to Foster Adherence to State Religious Neutrality. They said it would also provide a framework for requests for religious accommodations in certain bodies.

Alec Castonguay describes an interesting scene in his book *Philippe Couillard: la naissance d'un chef* (Philippe Couillard: The Birth of a Leader). Shortly after the Liberal leader learned he won a majority government in the 2014 general election while watching the election coverage in his hotel room, the news channel turns

---

[48] Sudha Krishnan and Benjamin Shingler, "Quebec bus drivers seek clarity on law that prohibits passengers from covering faces," *CBC News*, October 18, 2017, https://bit.ly/2rzzncN.

to Françoise David (at the time, founder and co-spokesperson of Quebec's fourth leading political party, Québec Solidaire). Couillard watched her make a public plea to put an end to the debate around religious symbols by adopting the Bouchard-Taylor recommendations once and for all. According to Castonguay, Couillard was moved by her appeal and vowed to take up this challenge in his first term in office.

I was struck by the poeticism of this story. Québec Solidaire is a left-leaning feminist and separatist party. While its leader and founder, David, is a highly respected politician and parliamentarian (she retired in January 2017), her party only won three seats in that election. What a victory for Quebec politics and Quebec people, I thought, if politicians from starkly opposing sides of the spectrum could work together to find a solution to the identity question. However, when I later asked Premier Couillard in a media scrum about seeing David on TV in 2014, he said he couldn't recall the moment that Castonguay described. I pushed him: could he not recall his motivation for introducing one of his government's defining pieces of legislation? Or had his motivation changed?

While David clearly called for the Bouchard-Taylor recommendations to be adopted,[49] the Liberals eventually rejected the idea. In 2008, the Bouchard-Taylor commission concluded that some public employees in positions of coercive authority should display religious neutrality in their functions—i.e. judges, Crown prosecutors, police officers, prison guards, and the speaker of the National Assembly. At the same time, the commission's final report suggested that teachers, students, health professionals, and public servants should be allowed to wear religious symbols. But

[49] At a national council in March 2019, Québec Solidaire membership rejected its traditional position on the Bouchard-Taylor recommendations. The party is now against any kind of ban on religious symbols.

the Liberals didn't see the need to ban symbols for anyone in any function, except for when it came to one piece of religious garb: the full face covering. Bill 62 ended up centering on just one issue: the right for Muslim women to receive public services while wearing a niqab.

The niqab was not a new issue in Quebec or Canadian politics—it factored largely as a campaign issue in the 2015 federal election.[50] However, with the passage of Bill 62, Quebec became the only jurisdiction in North America to ban Muslim face coverings in order to have access to public services. Section 10 of the bill stipulated the rules regarding religious face coverings:

> Personnel members of public bodies and of certain other bodies must exercise their functions with their face uncovered, unless they have to cover their face, in particular because of their working conditions or because of occupational or task-related requirements. In addition, persons receiving services from such personnel members must have their face uncovered.

Quebec's anglophone communities largely opposed the bill from the beginning. "When you don't have a problem, or you're not sick, maybe medication is not a good thing to take. So we're saying to ourselves, do we really need this?" said Stephen Burke, Central Quebec School Board chairman and executive member of the Quebec English School Board Association during public hearings for the bill. "We're worried about the divisiveness more than anything else. It creates a feeling of uneasiness and we can feel that," he said.

---

[50] Laura Payton, "Election Issues 2015: A Maclean's primer on the niqab," *Maclean's,* October 6, 2015, https://www.macleans.ca/politics/ottawa/election-issues-2015-a-macleans-primer-on-the-niqab/

The Liberals abandoned a transpartisan approach, and instead passed Bill 62 in October 2017 without any opposition support. Opposition parties wanted the bill to at least adopt the Bouchard-Taylor recommendations, with the CAQ pushing for teachers to be included in the list of employees that must show religious neutrality. The federal Liberal government also did not agree with the legislation. "I think I've been very clear that I don't think a government should be legislating what a woman should or shouldn't be wearing. I don't think that's something that is right for Canada," said Prime Minister Justin Trudeau.[51]

Other Quebecers wondered what the bill accomplished other than to deny public services, like taking a city bus or attending public school or college to a small number of Muslim women. In a particularly critical opinion piece published in *Chatelaine* magazine, Sadiya Ansari writes: "It's absurd to argue that these women—it's estimated that there are fewer than 100 of them—are a threat to Quebec's secular culture, but their image is powerful, because they represent the kind of difference some Quebecers are uncomfortable with."[52]

In another article for *Maclean's*, the province's anti-niqab law is referred to as "ludicrous claptrap that makes no sense."[53] Justice Minister Stéphanie Vallée first told reporters at the National Assembly that niqabi women would have to remove their face coverings to ride the city bus, but then contradicted herself multiple times. As *Maclean's* senior columnist Paul Wells (and other jour-

[51] Andy Blatchford (The Canadian Press), "Trudeau weighing options on Quebec face-covering ban in wake of court challenge," *Global News*, November 11, 2017, https://bit.ly/2q286zd.

[52] Sadiya Ansari, "Bill 62: In case you were wondering, this is what Islamophobia looks like," *Chatelaine*, November 20, 2017, https://bit.ly/2Q883MV.

[53] Paul Wells, "Why Quebec's Bill 62 is an indefensible mess," *Maclean's*, October 23, 2017, https://bit.ly/2q28yxp.

nalists) pointed out, the bill was riddled with contradictions—how could a law bar these women from riding the bus (where there was human interaction), but not the metro (where there was no human interaction)? Likewise, would riders also be barred for protecting their faces with scarves and balaclavas during Quebec's bitterly cold winters, or from wearing Halloween costumes?

Six days after the government passed the bill, including one full weekend of a media bonanza with Bill 62 making headlines across the country, a repentant Vallée held a press conference at the National Assembly to apologize for any "confusion" about the new law. Addressing a room full of journalists, the former lawyer and MNA for almost a decade said soberly, "I think it's important to clarify some issues, because over the weekend we heard all kinds of interpretations of the bill that are not [in line with what] the bill is all about." When one reporter told her she had contributed to the confusion, she adamantly replied, "I was coherent."

She explained that the law bans people from giving or receiving public services if their face is covered, except in the case of emergencies. In the case of riding the bus, the new law would only apply to seniors and students who need to show picture ID in order to qualify for a discount. There would be no sanctions for women who refuse to uncover, she said, rather services will be denied at the discretion of public employees. "Doesn't that put bus drivers, for instance, in an uncomfortable position of policing Muslim women who try to take public transportation with their faces still covered?" reporters asked.

"There are already procedures in place for bus drivers to intervene if a person refuses to respect the minimum rules to enter a bus," said Vallée. "As far as the burden on the bus driver is concerned, it's no different. It's normal that if someone comes with photo ID and glasses, we would ask them to take their glasses off," she gave as another example. Anyone affected can apply for religious accommodation, she added, but they will have to do so at each public service department and their request will be judged on a "case-by-case" basis.

Even as Bill 62 drew massive backlash, the Liberals defended it, arguing there was large support for a ban on face covers in Canada. An Ipsos poll conducted for Global News less than two weeks after Quebec adopted its niqab ban revealed that 68 percent of Canadians agreed with outlawing the Muslim face covering in their own provinces.[54] Global Montreal senior anchor Jamie Orchard pressed the premier on this issue during a year-end sit-down interview in December 2017.[55] Sitting across from Couillard, she expressed surprise at Bill 62.

The Premier responded that, "We did exactly what we said we would do."

Orchard persisted, asking him if he didn't think the issue of secularism and identity politics had become too divisive in Quebec. She pointed out that every time the issue of banning religious symbols comes up in the media, aggression towards women who wear Muslim veils increases. Wasn't it time for politicians to let this issue go?

"We cannot," Couillard replied. He suggested that francophone Quebecers (in contrast to the anglophone community he was speaking to via Orchard) feel more deeply about the identity debate. This doesn't prevent women from dressing the way they want outside, he argued, reiterating the fact that the law focuses on face coverings only during the giving or procurement of public services. Without directly addressing Orchard's point, Couil-

[54] Maham Abedi, "68 percent of Canadians want Quebec's face-coverings ban in their province," *Global News*, October 27, 2017, https://bit.ly/2NDVzuX.

[55] "Focus Montreal: Year-end interview with Philippe Couillard," *Global News*, December 29, 2017, https://bit.ly/2RyD9xU.

lard veered away from some of the answers he had commonly given in the past, and claimed that inaction on this issue would not be "well-received" in Quebec." This is a matter of importance for Quebecers, he said, paradoxically for many Quebecers who don't live day to day with diversity. "It always comes back to this idea of a minority people in North America surviving here, against all odds, for 400 years, he went on, saying that Quebecers have built a modern state and want it to stay that way. Sometimes, they see external influences as a threat, he explained. We could tell them they should not see those influences as a threat, "but it's very paternalistic to say this to people. This is how they believe it would affect us, so we have to answer that.[56]

Once Bill 62 was passed, a group of Muslim women mounted a legal challenge and Quebec's Superior Court suspended Section 10 of the law. In June 2018, another Superior Court judge upheld the original ruling, citing that the Quebec government was not able to provide adequate guidelines as to how the law should be implemented. After hundreds of hours studying the bill, Quebec's MNAs were right back where they started—in another election campaign with each political party clamouring to gain political points in a seemingly never-ending debate about identity.

---

[56] "Focus Montreal: Year-end interview with Philippe Couillard."

Chapter 4
The Charge of Racism

When the mosque re-opened in Quebec City a few days after the shooting, it allowed media in with cameras to film the damage. I was relieved not to be assigned to the story. I saw the video later that day: there were large bullet holes in the walls, several broken windows, and blood stains, many, many blood stains on the walls and the carpet. "It's our heart, this mosque, this mosque is the heart of our community here," said Mohamed Labidi, the mosque's former president. "We are attacked in our heart."

Rashad Wanas wasn't in the mosque that night, but the 38-year-old Iraqi immigrant later told Global News about the vicarious trauma he experienced because of it. He said that when he heard the news, he grabbed his wife and three children and hid inside a bedroom, fearing the shooter wouldn't stop after the mosque, but that more attacks were imminent. Wanas moved to Canada in 2011 after living through the Iraq war. News of the mosque attack took him back, to the time when he had live in hiding in Iraq. "I came to Canada," he said, "because I heard it was peaceful and safe, that life is good for families." After the attack, he began to fear for the safety of his family again, and especially for the safety of his wife, who wears a hijab. When his wife was setting off to work wearing her hijab, he told her not to, as "she might be targeted.[57]

Members of the Muslim community in Quebec City, particularly family members of victims who were born in Canada, shared the same shock that such an attack could take place here. In her victim impact letter, the daughter of Khaled Belkacemi, one of the six men killed in the mosque, wrote that her family moved to Canada because it was a place of "peace and stability."

Megda Belkacemi, the eldest of the seventeen children left orphaned by the shooting, explained that her parents fled a violent Algeria 30 years prior, They came to Canada, where they pursued their graduate studies and started a family. However, in 1992, during a period of extreme violence in Algeria, her parents moved back for work, bringing Belkacemi and her brother Amir with them. "The climate was terrifying. The terrorists targeted the Algerian elite: most notably, journalists, universities, writers," she said. Her parents were both employed at a university, and one day her father narrowly escaped death. The university rector, however, was assassinated the day her father had a meeting with him.

"He could have died that day .... The violence during this time forced my parents to make a choice for the safety of their children: quit their jobs and leave their families to return to Canada." As a result, she and her brother had a peaceful childhood, never expecting that as adults they would live in fear in Quebec. "How could a man who's the same age as me, that grew up in the same city as me, who has a similar education to me and whom I could have known ... how could this person kill my father and five other fathers?" she asked. When she arrived at the funeral home in Montreal, the sight of her father's body, she said, became

---

[57] Kelly Greig, "Quebec City man relives Iraq war horror after mosque attack," *Global News*, February 2, 2017, https://bit.ly/2E0hbvG.

an image she will never be able to erase from her memory: "There was no life in his body, there was a hole where his left eye should be because of the bullet in his head." His body was sent back to Algeria to be buried. "Alexandre Bissonnette was scared that his family would be attacked. And in the end, it was my family that was attacked."

Said Akjour was shot in the shoulder that night and, as a result, he missed eight months of work as he recovered. He testified during Bissonnette's sentencing hearing that he still had nightmares and fears for his personal safety in public, even at the grocery store or the library. His eight-year-old son refused to go back to the mosque and fears that his father will die. "What he went through, it was bad," Akjour said. "There is a life before January 29, 2017, and a life after."

Alexandre Bissonnette was never charged with terrorism (a decision members of Quebec City's mosque opposed publicly),[58] but there was no doubt that surviving victims, family members, and the wider Muslim population still feel targeted and terrorized. While a terrorism charge wouldn't have resulted in any difference to Bissonnette's sentence, the Muslim community felt it was important to draw attention to Islamophobia and hate crimes, which they say they experienced even before the attack.[59]

In September 2016, eight Muslims signed a letter to the Couillard government voicing their concerns. They specifically mentioned "acts of hatred" committed against Islamic centres in Saguenay, Montreal, Quebec City, Saint-Jean-sur-Richelieu, and Sherbrooke. They were concerned that hijabi women in particu-

[58] Evidence pointed to Bissonnette having acted as a lone wolf, rather than for a religious/ideological purpose or in order to promote a political agenda.
[59] In one of the first articles published about the attack, the *Global News* online team created a timeline of Islamophobic events against Quebec mosques dating back to 2012. Jesse Ferreras, "Anti-Muslim Incidents in Quebec: A Timeline," last modified January 30, 2017, https://bit.ly/2p7eCEk.

lar were in danger of harassment, and they also felt that police were not equipped to deal with growing online threats.

Shortly after the mosque shooting, Quebec City's Muslim community encountered another problem: there was no place to bury the victims. Five of the six victims' bodies were repatriated to their home countries. Megda Belkacemi's father, Khaled, was sent back to Algeria even though he had lived in Canada for more than thirty years, because Quebec City had no Muslim cemetery.[60]

The Quebec City Islamic Cultural Centre decided it would purchase land for a Muslim cemetery and by the summer of 2017, it had secured a plot of land about thirty-five kilometres outside of city limits in a small municipality called Saint-Apollinaire. Land in Quebec City is hard to find and expensive, so the deal between the mosque and a private landowner seemed like the best solution, but there was a problem. Even though the piece of land was situated behind an existing cemetery, it required a change to the zoning bylaw. Some opponents of the project argued that Quebec should be secular in matters of life *and* death and they objected to Muslims in the region being buried in separate cemeteries. Instead, they said Muslims should be buried in Islamic sections of existing cemeteries, side by side with their neighbours. They set about calling for a referendum.

After a long debate over whether or not municipalities should be stripped of their right to hold such referendums, the provincial government passed a law a month earlier in June 2017 that would have allowed the Saint-Apollinaire town council to deny a referendum, but the law hadn't yet received royal assent. And

[60] There were several Muslim cemeteries in the Greater Montreal area and a number of existing cemeteries have since added Muslim sections. Jesse Feith, "Two years after Quebec City's mosque attack, Muslim cemetery remains unbuilt," *The Gazette*, Montreal, last modified January 26, 2019, https://bit.ly/2NZIJpL.

thus, only a few dozen residents in total (in a community with a population of over 6,000 people) voted in the referendum on the zoning change: 16 people voted for and 19 voted against. With the difference of just three votes, Saint-Apollinaire had blocked the land sale for the Muslim cemetery.

"It's so flagrant it was a prejudiced vote," said Mohamed Kesri, the person responsible for the land deal for the Islamic Cultural Centre. The town's mayor agreed with him. "For an ordinary cemetery, I imagine it wouldn't have been a problem, but this is a Muslim cemetery. That's what created this conflict," Mayor Bernard Ouellet said at the time. He added that he heard that "people are afraid a mosque will be next" and that Muslim people would start buying houses in the area and "invade."

Blocking a private land sale in order to prevent the community from building its own cemetery after six of its members were shot to death in cold blood earlier that year inevitably made national headlines. Even Mayor Ouellet had trouble defending it, saying he was aware that people from outside of Quebec would view his town (and perhaps small-town Quebec, in general) as racist and xenophobic.

Kesri insisted that the mosque was going to fight the decision. It was going to hire a lawyer and seek justice—unless, he said, another mayor called in the meantime and offered to sell a parcel of land.

The Dark Side of Quebec's Identity Crisis

In the days following the attack, Quebec society was characterized as a breeding ground for racist and Islamophobic sentiment. "My gut reaction to the news was 'That's not us!' I tweeted it," Lise Ravary wrote in the *National Post*. "Replies from other commenters came fast and furious. 'Oh yes, it is. Quebec is a racist society. Islamophobia and anti-Semitism are rampant.'"[61] Even RCMP Commissioner Bob Paulson expressed his fears about the current political rhetoric. "There is, and I believe everyone will agree with me, a more scathing tone in the political discourse that seems to attract, agitate, and radicalize people of all backgrounds—particularly those which don't know anything about it. That concerns us enormously," he said.[62]

Private Quebec City radio stations, commonly referred to as *radio-poubelle* (trash radio) were also accused of having some responsibility for the tragedy because they routinely allowed their hosts to make Islamophobic comments on air.[63] In an interview with Radio-Canada (RDI), the French CBC, Michel Juneau-Katsuya, former CSIS intelligence officer and manager went so far as to say that some Quebec City radio hosts had "blood on their hands." *La Presse*, which also quoted Juneau-Katsuya, gave one glaring example:

> In December (2017), the press council received a complaint against Radio X and its host Dominic Maurais for racist remarks made with co-host Jacques Brassard in 2015. 'If all Muslims are not terrorists at present, all terrorists are Muslims. Isn't that right?' Jacques Brassard asked. And Dominic Maurais endorsed the co-hosts comments by responding, 'Yes.'[64]

---

[61] Lise Ravary, "It took a massacre in a mosque, but Quebecers now see the darkest side of their identity crisis," *National Post*, February 1, 2017, https://bit.ly/2pT4Ypt.

[62] Audrey Ruel-Manseau, "La GRC 'preoccupée' par le ton du discours politique," *La Presse*, February 7, 2017, https://bit.ly/2qGVX2M.

[63] Louise Leduc and Louis-Samuel Perron, "Radios de Québec: l'heure est à la prudence." *La Presse*, February 1, 2017, https://bit.ly/2CL5cSp.

[64] Louise Leduc and Louis-Samuel Perron, "Radios de Québec."

A blog called *Sortons les radio-poubelles* ("Take out trash radio") has been keeping track of some of the most egregious examples of Islamophobic comments on Quebec City's airwaves since 2012:

"The gang that is openly at war against the West and our values are the Muslims .... I'm afraid that in five, ten years, we will have problems here," host Jeff Fillion said on Radio-Pirate on December 9, 2015.

"They (Muslims) abhor Western values, liberty, democracy, equality between men and women. They want to destroy our civilization," said Jacques Brassard on Radio X on September 19, 2016.

In the summer of 2016, someone had dropped a pig's head at the doorstep of the Quebec City Islamic Cultural Centre with a note reading "Bon appétit." Eric Duhaime, host at FM93, said on air about the incident: "Where is it written in the criminal code that I don't have the right to give (someone) a pig head? It's maybe a silly joke .... It's a little ridiculous .... But where is the hate?"[65]

"Jacques Brassard is not just anyone, he's a former PQ minister," said Étienne Lanthier,[66] spokesperson for the coalition that runs Sortons les radio-poubelles. "These are people who have a lot of influence over their followers."

In the immediate days following the shooting, some media commentators offered what could be interpreted as an apology. Lise Ravary wrote,

> As a conservative columnist at war with religious extremism and political Islam in particular, I will keep myself in check. When denouncing Islamism, I always insist that my

[65] Tête de porc ensanglantée au centre islamique : « En quoi c'est de la haine? », demande Duhaime: https://sortonslespoubelles.com/tete-de-porc-ensanglantee-au-centre-islamique-en-quoi-cest-de-la-haine-demande-duhaime/

[66] Étienne Lanthier is not his real name. The coalition does not release its members' names publicly out of fear of reprisal.

> comments do not apply to Muslims as a people or to Islam as a faith. I realized last Sunday that many readers don't see the difference, some because they can't. Others because they won't. Media must take this into consideration.[67]

Quebec City radio host Sylvain Bouchard said,

> We have to fight against disinformation and I didn't do that enough. Sometimes there were things that circulated from the extreme right, racists or Islamaphobes and I had the tendency to say, 'People don't believe that! Do we really need to talk about that?' Yes! Yes, I should have. We should have given more information about the Muslim religion.

Premier Philippe Couillard also called for a change in the tone of political rhetoric: "Words can hurt. Words can be knives slashing at people's consciousness," he said. However, Lanthier says that when it came to Quebec City radio hosts, there was "no mea culpa" and since the mosque attack, he says he's seen no improvement. Hosts continue to spout Islamophobic rhetoric over the airwaves. "There are no consequences; it's total impunity, even after the attack," Lanthier said. "The shooting was a great revelation for a lot of people … there was a door that opened and then quickly shut again. Nothing has changed."

Other media commentators defended Quebec, claiming it is no more intolerant than the rest of Canada. "Anti-Muslim sentiment is hardly relegated to Quebec," writes Supriya Dwivedi.[68] In fact, the number of hate crimes reported to police across Canada where Muslims were the target tripled between 2012, when po-

---

[67] Ravary, "It took a massacre in a mosque."

[68] Dwivedi Supriya, "Quebec and Canada have an Islamophobia problem," *Global News*, February 2, 2017, https://bit.ly/2X4bBRP.

lice recorded 45 of these crimes, and 2015, when police recorded 159. This represented an increase of 253 percent. By 2017, that number had risen again with 349 incidents reported to police, an increase of 151 percent over 2016. According to Statistics Canada, Jewish people were the biggest targets for hate crimes, while Muslims were targeted for more violent crimes, such as "uttering threats," common assault, and assault with a weapon or aggravated assault.[69]

However, there continues to be a debate in Quebec over whether or not Islamophobia even exists. In 2019, the city of Toronto declared January 29 a day of remembrance and action on Islamophobia, but Quebec Premier Francois Legault rejected the idea, as he had in the past. Just two days after the second anniversary of the mosque shooting, the newly-elected Premier denied there was a problem at all. Indeed, he took this same position during the debate to hold public consultations on systemic racism. "There is no Islamophobia in Quebec," Legault told reporters.

The National Council of Canadian Muslims called on Legault to retract the remarks, and the president of the Quebec City Islamic Cultural Centre, Boufeldja Benabdallah, responded almost immediately in a public letter addressed to the premier: "I appeal to your generosity and your intelligence to remain the premier for all Quebecers, and not just those who elected you, to ensure this wound doesn't become an insurmountable fracture that your government will be responsible for." he wrote.

Benabdallah also noted that the Quebec City mosque has been the target of other Islamophobic acts: swastikas painted on the walls, a pig's head left at its entrance during Ramadan, and excrement flung at the door. In August 2017, the mosque's former

---

[69] Jesse Ferreras, "In Canada, Jews face more hate crimes, while Muslims face more violent ones: StatCan," *Global News*, November 30, 2018, https://bit.ly/2X3mHGI.

president's car was set on fire.[70]

The next day, the premier's office sought to nuance his comments in a statement: "Unfortunately, there are still too many racist acts that occur in our society. However, there is no trend or culture of Islamophobia in Quebec. Quebecers are open and tolerant and will continue to exhibit these qualities." Ironically, a 49-year-old Laval man, Pierre Dion, appeared in court the very day Legault released this statement. He faced two charges of inciting hatred for a video he published that praised Quebec City's mosque shooter and expressed hatred toward Muslims. He was later sentenced to thirty days in prison.[71]

Islamophobia does exist in Quebec, as it exists elsewhere. But if what the premier was trying to say was that Islamophobic events were isolated incidents that don't represent Quebec society on the whole, there is ample evidence of that, too.

A few weeks after the Saint-Apollinaire land deal was blocked, the mayor of Quebec City called an unexpected press conference. As the National Assembly reporter, I cover city hall only when something major happens, but journalists know that a news conference called late on a Friday—and right before the mayor is scheduled to go on holidays—is to announce something major. We packed up our gear and headed to the Hôtel de Ville.

Mayor Régis Labaume was joined by two now-recognizable leaders from the mosque, Mohamed Labidi and Boufeldja Benabdallah. In the days following the fatal shooting and the media frenzy that ensued, the mosque—run by volunteers—needed a spokesperson. Labidi and Benabdallah stood up to represent their community. "I decided to pick up the baton and fight against

[70] Morgan Lowrie (The Canadian Press), "François Legault backtracks on Islamophobia comment after outcry by Muslim groups," *Global News*, February 1, 2019, https://bit.ly/2NFeeqi.

[71] Valérie Gonthier, "30 jours de prison pour le «troll» Pierre Dion," *TVA Nouvelles*, June 11, 2019, https://bit.ly/2NBiRBu.

ignorance," Benabdallah, an Algerian immigrant who's lived in Quebec City for almost fifty years, told me once when I asked him how he felt about being an unintentional leader.

The three men were seated side by side as the Quebec City mayor announced that he had a found a solution for the land needed to build the city's first Muslim cemetery and that he was more than pleased it would be within city limits. The city would accept, he said, an offer similar to what the Islamic Cultural Centre had been willing to pay for the Saint-Apollinaire deal—$270,000 for 5,706 square metres next to the existing Belmont cemetery.

"Every human being has the right to choose a burial place in dignity and in harmony with their personal beliefs," Mayor Labeaume said. He added that the land was already zoned for a cemetery and so the Muslim community would not have to jump through any more hoops. The land was theirs. "For more than 400 years, Quebec has welcomed people from all cultures, languages and religions," Labeaume said. "To live together, no matter our origins, is fundamental for our society to succeed." The mosque leaders broke down in tears of gratitude, relieved that Quebec Muslims would now be able to "die in peace," they explained.

Having covered this news story from the start, I too felt justice had been served. It was a perfect narrative: after an unthinkable tragedy, the community fought for a place to ensure members of the community had a choice in burial grounds. In doing so, they encountered both support and discrimination. They overcame Islamophobia to finally secure the land for a Muslim cemetery and now we could turn the page. I knew I was being optimistic, but that's what I wanted—for this story to end here, with the joy and relief emanating from that media room in city hall, with the collaboration between a community and its municipal government. That first weekend in August, heading into the second half of summer, I pressed pause on the mosque shooting story for several days and forgot about the upcoming trial for the shooter.

The Fight over Religious Symbols

On the morning of Wednesday, March 28, 2018, I arrived at court early, with butterflies in my stomach. I was so nervous—I had never covered a first-degree murder trial before, let alone a murder trial of this magnitude. I had overestimated the time it would take us to prepare, load our gear up in the truck, drive to the courthouse, re-read my notes, and get through security. In the line, I recognized the same members of the mosque and other journalists who had been there on Monday, when we all came to hear the accused enter his plea.

Two days earlier, we sat in court while the judge read out the names of all the victims, and Bissonnette pleaded not guilty to six counts of first degree murder and again to six counts of attempted murder, five for the people he shot and critically injured and one for the 35 other people in the mosque that night (31 men and four children). Believing that what would follow would be mostly procedural, there were far fewer of us in the courtroom when pre-trial motions continued after a long recess for lunch. Only a handful of journalists remained to hear Bissonnette tell the judge he had changed his mind—he wanted to plead guilty. "I've thought about this a long time. In my heart, this is the decision I've made," Bissonnette told the judge. But the judge wasn't ready to accept Bissonnette's new plea. He ordered him to undergo a psychiatric evaluation and court would resume two days later. Until then, everything that happened would remain under a publication ban.

Now the courtroom was packed. I found a seat and saved the one beside me for a colleague who had come up from Montreal. He came in a few minutes later, and I waved him over; he sat down and tried to balance his iPad on his lap. It was going to be cramped. I looked around to see who I might have interviewed before and whose names I remembered. Families sat together and looked oddly calm, I thought. If Bissonnette goes ahead with entering a guilty plea, that will mean survivors and family members will not have to sit through a two-month long trial, or even longer. The closure they had been waiting over a year for could come today. I couldn't imagine what that must feel like.

Finally, the judge entered, and the court was called to order. Testimony from the psychiatrist confirmed that the accused was of sound mind and Bissonnette reiterated, without faltering, his desire to change his plea. The judge took a deep sigh. He then began to re-read the charges against him. With each count, he was careful to pronounce correctly the name of the victim killed or injured by Bissonnette's firearm. The butterflies in my stomach quickly turned to aches. With each name read aloud, hollowly into the microphone, the families and the friends of that person consequently let out loud sobs, which I realized they'd been holding inside this whole time. What I had mistakenly perceived as calm had been an inability to breathe. Each new name allowed more and more heavy sobs to evacuate the lungs of the grieving. By the twelfth count, Bissonnette had admitted to the atrocities committed against 46 people.

I was wrong about the closure though. There was no trial, but rather a sentencing hearing that proceeded for more than three weeks. After pleading guilty, Bissonnette read aloud a letter in which he said he is "neither a terrorist nor an Islamophobe." As for his motive, he offered little explanation: "I am ashamed. Ashamed of what I did," he read. "I do not know why I committed such an insane act and, still today, I have trouble believing it .... I had been having suicidal thoughts and ideas and an obsession with death for a long time. It's as though I was battling a demon that finished by winning out."

The hearing was emotionally trying for the victims and families of the deceased. Those who could stand to watch it stayed to view graphic surveillance video of Bissonnette's execution-style killings, as well as police interrogation video where Bissonnette said he targeted the mosque because he believed some of the worshipers were Islamist terrorists. As journalists, we were fixated on every word. I frantically wrote down notes and returned home every evening trying to make sense of what I'd heard. Mental health and depression, hate, ignorance—what was the real reason behind the attack? Could it have been prevented?

While I was at court, the National Assembly was still in session and religious accommodations were still an issue of debate. Out of habit, I continued to read the political stories coming out of the press tribune. The day after the court viewed the video of the shooting, another religious symbols debate erupted.

The subject of this debate was a 17-year-old Muslim police studies student who had been profiled in one of the French-language newspapers.[72] Sondos Lamrhari was an athletic, well-spoken, and determined teenager who was clearly not afraid to be at the centre of a contentious issue. She was the first police studies student to wear the hijab and hoped to become the first police officer in Quebec to do so. Not if the PQ or the CAQ formed the next majority government, the two opposition parties said. They came out in reaction to Lamrhari's interview.

"The opposition Coalition Avenir Québec says a police car is not a place of worship and an officer in uniform cannot serve the state and God at the same time," I read in a Canadian Press arti-

[72] Dominique Scali, "Determinée à être policière et à conserver son voile," *Le Journal de Montréal*, April 12, 2018, https://bit.ly/2NEYyTC.

cle.[73] During Question Period, Justice Minister Stéphanie Vallée made an emotional appeal: "Don't crush the dreams of a young 17-year-old girl," she said.

Politicians were still talking about Lamrhari's hijab when victims began to take the stand at Bissonnette's sentencing hearing. While MNAs debated banning religious symbols, victims testified to a much greater political issue: the discrimination they experienced. One man who took the stand said he didn't understand prejudiced attitudes against immigrants, because newcomers to Quebec are almost always educated and qualified to start working here. He referred to Canada's immigrant class as an unrecognized "elite" comprising individuals who are chronically underemployed because their international credentials are not recognized.

When Benabdallah took the stand, he told the judge that Muslims in Quebec are neither violent nor radicalized, but that they are sometimes treated as if they are connected to events happening elsewhere in the world. "We are Quebec and Canadian citizens; why do I have to explain what happened in Iraq and Iran?" he asked rhetorically.

At a vigil held to mark the one-year anniversary of the shooting, Prime Minister Justin Trudeau told a crowd gathered outside the mosque, "No matter our faith or where we were born, we are equal members of this country. We will not let an act of intolerance divide us and make any Canadian feel less at home." But Benabdallah, and others who testified, felt strongly to the contrary. They said that Muslim Canadians often feel marginalized from the rest of society, and that the shooting only reinforced this sense of isolation. One year later, attendance at the Quebec City Islamic Cultural Centre was down one third of what it was before

---

[73] The Canadian Press, "Aspiring police recruit's hijab demand heats up Quebec religious accommodation debate," *Ottawa Citizen*, April 12, 2018, https://bit.ly/2O1QL1j.

the shooting.

Reading from a prepared letter, Benabdallah said to Bissonnette: "I want you to know that you have killed the precious moments of friendship and fraternity .... And these children who ran and laughed carefree. They saw adults fall from the gunfire, their bodies full of bullets—how are they ever going to forget that?"

Would Quebecers forget?

Chapter 5
The Mosque Shooting

When Alexandre Bissonnette, the 28-year-old former political science student, abruptly changed his plea in March 2018 and confessed to shooting and killing six men and injuring nineteen others in a mosque during evening prayers, we thought, maybe now, we'll finally find out what drove a young man to commit such an unimaginable atrocity in a place of worship. For over a year, the question, "*Why did this happen?*" haunted not only the grieving Quebec City Muslim community, but all residents, including myself and other journalists who covered the attack from the beginning.

Since the mosque shooting on that frigid evening in January 2017, the debate came up frequently about whether or not Quebec's *Capitale-Nationale*, considered to be one of the safest cities in the country, is more racist or Islamophobic than other cities in Canada. I moved to the provincial capital when I got the job as the National Assembly reporter for Global News in 2016, and there are a few things I've noticed. Unlike the Montreal metropolis, which is one of the most culturally diverse cities in Canada, the rest of Quebec, including Quebec City, is strikingly less diverse. But that is changing. I take the bus to work almost every day and see many representatives of visible minorities among my fellow passengers. This immigration is a relatively recent development in Quebec City.[74] There are numerous examples of minority newcomers integrating successfully into the fabric of society, but sadly, sometimes change also fuels hostility.

As discussed in Chapter Four, radio commentators, politicians, and everyday Quebecers express hostility, especially towards Muslims, publicly. Did this contribute to the 2017 Quebec City mosque shooting?

Expert Testimony

Victims and their families were spared the torment of a trial, but prosecutors still combed through the evidence, methodically and completely, during a four-week sentencing hearing. It was gut-wrenching. And on more than one occasion I felt like we would never understand why this happened.

During the hearing, four experts (two psychiatrists and a forensic psychologist for the defence, as well as a psychologist for the Crown), presented detailed reports, revealing numerous unknown facts about the shooter's childhood, medical and psychiatric history, and his plans of suicide and murder. They testified that Bissonnette was cooperative with them and willingly answered their questions. They did not claim, however, that he never lied. For months during his incarceration he pretended to hear voices, something he later told prison social worker Guylaine Cayouette he'd made up.

---

[74] In fact, on its immigration website, the Government of Quebec points out that this growing diversity is a result of fewer immigrants being selected from "traditional pools from Western Europe" and more often coming from the Middle East, North Africa, the West Indies, and Central America. "Diversité ethnoculturelle au Québec," Immigration Québec, https://bit.ly/33DI57R.

"I could have killed anyone. I wasn't targeting Muslims," he told her. "I wanted glory." He continued, "I regret not killing more people. The victims are in heaven and I live in hell. I want to plead guilty. I told my lawyer and my parents. My parents support me. I did research on serial killers and they are my idols." He told her he was tired of playing a role, saying, "It's not true that I don't remember anything. I remember it all." The experts agreed Bissonnette knew what he was doing.[75]

"Was this racist? Totally racist, even if (Bissonnette) doesn't see it ... it's clear it was based on something completely false ... [but] this crime was too egotistical to be a terrorist act .... This is someone who was seeking revenge ... life was hard and painful ... and for once in his life he could be powerful, famous," said Dr. Gilles Chamberland, a psychologist for the Crown.[76]

On the morning of January 29, 2017, Alexandre Bissonnette woke up in the apartment he shared with his twin brother. He took a quick shower, made himself breakfast, and pulled up the *New York Times* website on his laptop.[77] As he read stories about Donald Trump's Muslim ban, he wished he did not have to return to work the next day. For the last month, he'd been on medical leave from his part-time job at the Quebec City blood bank. He was too depressed, too anxious to work. Too depressed to enroll for the winter semester at Laval University. He didn't think he could work and live independently, even if his parents wanted him to. "It's as if it wasn't important anymore. I abandoned everything," he explained after his arrest.

Six months before the shooting, his parents had pushed the

[75] Information for this chapter come from my own notes and from documents provided to reporters in court during Alexandre Bissonnette's sentencing hearing.

[76] Dr. Gilles Chamberland testified in court on April 26, 2018.

[77] A report of Bissonnette's search history was presented during court proceedings.

27-year-old fraternal twins out of the house in an effort to force their sons to become independent, but instead Bissonnette says his anxiety only increased while living on his own. He also worried constantly that the police would come and take away the guns his parents let him store at their house. He had been prescribed the anti-depressant Paxil, but he contemplated suicide, something he hid from his parents, as well as the authorities. Bissonnette had been a licensed gun owner for several years, but he had lied on his application form that he had no history of psychiatric problems, nor any suicidal thoughts. The truth was he once bought a handgun and he tried to take his life numerous times. He was mad at himself that he couldn't go through with it.

Then, on November 26, 2016, two months before the mosque shooting, Bissonnette put two handguns and fifty bullets in his backpack and drove to Quebec City's Place Laurier, one of the largest shopping malls in Canada. He got out of his vehicle and loaded one of the pistols in the parking lot, then changed his mind. But before driving away, he noticed a security camera.

On that cold Sunday morning on January 29, he had become convinced someone had seen him on the security footage and the police would soon come and arrest him. He was sure that this day was his last chance to carry out his plan. He left the apartment to buy food and a 750 ml bottle of sake. By early afternoon, Bissonnette started drinking while he continued to search the Internet on his laptop. He looked up the Twitter profiles of American TV personalities Ann Coulter and Bill O'Reilly. On Facebook, he looked at the page of far-right French presidential candidate Marine Le Pen. Then, as he had many times that month, he returned to the pages of James Gamble and Justin Bourque. Gamble killed himself in 2015, before allegedly planning a mass shooting at the Halifax Shopping Centre. Bourque shot five New Brunswick RCMP officers, killing three in 2014.

Bissonnette felt "connected" to mass shooters, beginning with an interest in the Columbine when he was 15. He began listening to heavy metal, the same music as the Columbine shooters. "It was like an obsession, the thing that interested me the most in life ... It gave my life meaning," he told psychiatrist Dr. Marie-Frédérique Allard.[78]

Bissonnette said he was picked on as a child because he was smaller, had many allergies, asthma and a persistent cough. He admitted that he never had a relationship with a woman beyond a "few one-night stands." One of his former teachers testified that, in high school, the daily bullying became physically violent: in at least one incident, bigger kids grabbed him by the collar and shoved him up against the lockers. Lucie Côté, who was Bissonnette's teacher in two different years at two different schools, said he developed reflexes of nervousness and fear and did not defend himself. "Alexandre is not a monster," she testified. Bissonnette admitted that, at the time, he imagined killing his harassers and burning the school down.

In August 2014, Bissonnette tried to hang himself in the back shed of his parent's house, but his brother was at home, and he couldn't bring himself to go through with it. He told forensic psychologist, Marc-André Lamontagne, who testified for the Crown, he believes "that's when things took a sinister turn." The idea of "just" killing himself wasn't enough. The idea of committing a mass shooting felt exciting. "I was, like, obsessed by the power that gave them [mass killers]."[79]

By the summer of 2015, the idea of suicide became "more ur-

[78] Dr. Marie-Frédérique Allard prepared an assessment of the danger Bissonnette presented which she submitted to his defence council on April 11, 2018; the report was later presented as evidence in court.

[79] Marc-André Lamontagne prepared a psychological evaluation of the danger and risk of violent recidivism, which was submitted to the Crown on April 16, 2018.

gent" as he swung between feelings of hopelessness and anger. "I needed to do something big before I committed suicide, even if there was a part of me that didn't want to .... I needed to do something with my life. You can't waste yourself like that," he later told Lamontagne. "You're not going to let yourself die a nobody."

However, he felt as though he couldn't carry out a mass murder of individuals he considered innocent. And, as it turned out, there were some people he felt he could target without hesitation. At the end of December 2016, he unintentionally drove by the Quebec City Islamic Cultural Centre. He had become interested in the American election and began reading more about immigration and Islamist terrorism. If he chose the mosque in the city's Saint-Foy neighbourhood as his future target, he thought, then maybe he could eliminate a dangerous fanatic or a terrorist.

In his interrogation video, the court heard Bissonnette tell investigators he wanted to protect his family from terrorist attacks. Instead of shooting himself "alone in the woods," Bissonnette said, thanks to his actions, "maybe 100 people will now be saved .... Maybe 200 or 300 people." For the next month, Bissonnette routinely googled the mosque and looked at the Quebec City Islamic Cultural Centre's Facebook page. He saved floor plans of the mosque on his laptop.

Evening of January 29, 2017

On January 29, he made those same searches again. That evening, he drove to his parents' house for what he described as "his last supper," He could feel the effects of the alcohol he'd been drinking all afternoon, but he didn't let his parents see he was drunk. While there, he visited *The Guardian*, ABC, and CBC news websites, watched Youtube videos of Ed Sheeran and the Glock 17 handgun. And, once again, he visited James Gamble's Facebook page. However, Bissonnette would later tell the police interrogator it was a tweet from Justin Trudeau that made him "lose it."

The Prime Minister was responding to Donald Trump's travel ban, the U.S. president's plan to restrict immigration from Muslim majority countries like Iran, Libya, Somalia, Syria, and Yemen. (The ban also included non-Muslim majority countries like North Korea and Venezuela). Welcoming refugees and other immigrants to Canada, Trudeau had tweeted, "To those fleeing persecution, terror & war, Canadians will welcome you, regardless of your faith. Diversity is our strength #WelcomeToCanada."

Within an hour, Bissonnette got his rifle from his bedroom downstairs. He placed it and two illegal 30-bullet magazines in a soft guitar case. He put a 9mm Glock handgun in his pocket. He told his parents he was going to the gun range and thought, "I'm never coming back home."

Sometime after 7 p.m., Bissonnette heard his cell phone ring. It was his father calling to say the gun range was closed. Bissonnette told him that he was going to make a stop at the grocery store before heading back to the house. "Why don't you come home right now?" his father asked. Bissonnette snapped back that his father should stop trying to control him and tell him what to do. This angry exchange only made him more determined to follow through with his plan. However, by the time he drove to the mosque, Bissonnette again began to hesitate. He parked on a side road near an apartment building where he looked up the prayer times online. There were dozens of people inside at that very minute. He thought, "I can't do this."

He drove to a nearby convenience store where he purchased a Vodka Ice and drank it at once. He drove back to the Islamic Cultural Centre and sat in his car. He was starting to feel more uninhibited because of the alcohol. When a passerby walked by his car, Bissonnette was convinced he should act fast. If the stranger had seen him with his guns, which he was sure was the case, he would soon be reported and arrested. "I no longer had an exit. I told myself, 'Go!'"

Inside the mosque, prayers had finished and many worshippers were standing around talking and laughing together. Four children played quietly together in the corner. Outside, Bissonnette approached the front entrance of the mosque on foot, a .223 semi-automatic rifle in his hands. He fired at his first two victims. Ibrahima Barry and Mamodou Tanou Barry were taken by surprise in the icy cold. The men fell to the ground as the rifle jammed. Bissonnette then removed the handgun from his pocket and shot victims again at close range. "I was searching for control. At least in these last moments of my life, I was going to be like God. I was going to decide life or death. After being tormented, at least once in my life *I* would have the big end of the stick," Bissonnette told Lamontagne.

The sound of gunshots sent the people inside the mosque running in panic. When Bissonnette entered the building, they ran from the bullets towards a small back room, the only shelter available in the large open prayer space. But Azzedine Soufiane, a local butcher shop owner, stayed calm. Soufiane was known as a friend and mentor for many newcomers and members of Quebec City's Muslim community. In those first frightful seconds as they saw a lone shooter come towards them, he caught the eye of Dr. Merouane Rachidi. "It is just a single person, we shouldn't be afraid," Soufiane said. He then dove towards the assassin, attempting to knock him to the ground and nearly forcing him to drop his gun. But as Bissonnette broke free of his grasp, Soufiane was unable to escape his gunfire. "The people who were shot that night were the best among us," Ibrahim Sbai testified in court.

In less than two minutes, Bissonnette had reloaded his firearm twice. Of the 50 handgun cartridges he had with him that night, he fired off forty-eight, killing six men, and seriously injuring five others. Ahmed Cheddadi, another witness, later told the Quebec City courtroom: "I will never forget how this cold-blooded individual shot at everyone ... I will never forget the images of blood, of death, of bodies after the carnage .... He is a monster who terrorized a whole community—the whole city—killing in a place of worship."

Bissonnette ran out of the mosque back to his car and started driving. He wanted to kill himself. He wanted to drive to Charlevoix, a place he used to go camping as a child. He would lay down on the ground and stare up at the stars and then he'd kill himself. Finally.[80]

But the effects of the alcohol were wearing off. Fourteen minutes after the massacre, Bissonnette changed his mind. On the highway to Charlevoix, Bissonnette was still in city limits when he called 9-1-1. He threatened several times to shoot himself in the head while speaking with the 9-1-1 operator but, after staying on the line for fifty minutes, the operator convinced Bissonnette to leave his handgun on the back seat, wait for police, and surrender.

In June 2018, Bissonnette's parents made a brief statement to media in defence of their son, whom they described as a mentally-ill victim of life-long bullying. "All our efforts to end the bullying failed," said Raymond Bissonnette. "The Crown said that all young people are bullied sometime in their lives and don't commit serious crimes. I think this opinion does not do justice to the serious damage and suffering caused by bullying and intimidation."

Bissonnette was sentenced to life in prison with no chance of parole for forty years.

---

[80] This was revealed in Dr. Marie-Frédérique Allard's report.

After the Tragedy

In the hours following the attack, Quebec City mayor Régis Labeaume, Premier Philippe Couillard, and Public Security Minister Martin Coiteux jointly held an emotional press conference in the middle of the night, telling Quebec Muslims, "We love you," and "We are with you." Later the next day, Prime Minister Justin Trudeau spoke in the House of Commons, saying, "This was a group of innocents targeted for practising their faith. Make no mistake—this was a terrorist attack. It was an attack on our most intrinsic and cherished values as Canadians—values of openness, diversity, and freedom of religion."

The outpouring of support for Quebec City's Muslim community was touching. A vigil for the victims was quickly organized, and thousands of people, including the Prime Minister, assembled in the parking lot of a church adjacent to the mosque and marched in solidarity with the victims and their families. I couldn't feel my fingertips because I had put my hand-warmers in my coat pocket to try to keep my cell phone battery from dying. It was hard to hold back my emotions at the sight of so many people—and so many flowers and cards and posters—on one of the coldest nights of the year. Maybe things would change.

Premier Couillard offered more hope in his speech at the second of two funerals for the victims (the first was held in Montreal for three of the victims, followed by another service for the other victims in Quebec City the next day). He addressed the crowd of thousands gathered in the Quebec City Convention Centre with *As-salamu alaykum* ("peace be upon you," in Arabic). "I repeat these words purposely because in movies, they are associated with terrorists," he said.

Earlier that morning, he promised to immediately address "violent racism" in Quebec. He vowed to temporarily suspend work on his government's religious neutrality bill, Bill 62, while offering to add an amendment that would prohibit government employees from covering their faces. He hoped this would convince opposition parties to unanimously adopt the bill without further divisive debate. "Unanimity here, in this present time, would be a very positive signal in our society," he said. The premier also condemned US President Donald Trump and federal Conservative party candidate Kellie Leitch, who he said were using the mosque attack as justification to tighten immigration, even though the alleged gunman was Canadian. "Where's the logic? I don't understand. People are just turning the table around here. What's at [the root] cause here is racism and xenophobia," Premier Couillard said.

An Angus Reid Institute survey conducted two weeks after the attack found that attitudes had become incrementally more positive towards Canada's Muslim communities. 46 percent of Canadians still viewed Islam unfavourably, but in Quebec, the number of people who said they viewed the Islamic faith more favourably had more than doubled since 2009, a jump from 15 percent to 32 percent.[81] The Angus Reid Institute's executive director, Shachi Kurl suggested the mosque shooting might explain it.

"Quebecers themselves were very shaken by the event. We did see leadership come out very quickly," he said. "We saw Premier Philippe Couillard, the Mayor of Quebec City, and others come out very strongly and say Muslims are Quebecers. We are all in this together. Messages of harmony, messages of support and togetherness for the Muslim community."

Another debate, however, would soon call that message of harmony into question once again.

---

[81] Adam Frisk, "Nearly half of Canadians view Islam unfavourably, survey finds," *Global News*, April 4, 2017, https://bit.ly/2NXbZxm.

Chapter 6
Populism and the Donald Trump of Quebec

Every year in July, Quebec City plays host to an eleven-day outdoor music festival on the Plains of Abraham. One Saturday evening, my boyfriend and I were lazing around the house when we heard music. It was one of the opening acts for that night's headliner, Shawn Mendes. Our house is almost fourteen kilometres away from the festival grounds, but the music was clear enough for us to make out some of the lyrics. It was a particularly windy evening and I wondered if that had anything to do with it.

"No, it's because of the river," my boyfriend suggested. The St. Lawrence River, Quebec's most defining geographical feature, creates a large, open space that carries scents and sounds north for miles. This was fascinating. As a political journalist always on the hunt for an apt metaphor, I could already see how this natural phenomenon would come in handy as an analogy for how ideas and movements making a lot of noise in one part of the world can waft up to another part and sound like it's resonating there too.

Even after the mosque shooting, the issues of identity, immigration, and nationalism continued to dominate the 2018 Quebec election campaign. And after facing a historic defeat, the Liberal

Party even reflected on whether or not it needed to adopt a more nationalist tone in order to win back its popular support, particularly among francophone voters.[82] After Philippe Couillard stepped down, Interim Liberal Leader Pierre Arcand told reporters that it's possible, when you're in government, to forget what the people want. "In opposition," he said, Liberals will "have more time to reflect on what the population really wants."[83]

Arcand seemed to be acknowledging that this was in fact what Coalition Avenir Québec (CAQ) leader, François Legault, had succeeded in doing. Legault first proposed the idea of lowering the threshold for immigrants to Quebec as leader of the second opposition during the 2016 American presidential election. The timing was alarming and had some critics calling Legault "Quebec's Donald Trump."[84] Many people feared that the anti-immigration rhetoric from the real estate tycoon-turned-presidential candidate was encouraging populist and racist attitudes across North America. Indeed, Ontario Tech University professors maintained that,

> His campaign and his surprising electoral victory rode a wave of anti-elitism and xenophobia .... His rhetoric touched a chord, and in fact emboldened and energized white supremacist ideologies, identities, movements and practices in the United States and around the world .... [And] the Trump Effect touched Canada as well."[85]

Legault, himself a millionaire businessman (he co-founded Air

[82] Jonathan Plamondon, "Pour un nationalisme inclusif de dialogue," *La Presse*, October 29, 2018, https://bit.ly/2K8l9WE.
[83] Raquel Fletcher, "Quebec's Liberals want to re-engage with average voters," *Global News*, October 25, 2018, https://bit.ly/33FfgrH.
[84] Mathieu Dion, "François Legault, le Donald Trump du Québec?" Radio-Canada, November 11, 2016, video, https://bit.ly/33JTVxy.
[85] Perry et al., "The Dangers of Porous Borders," 53.

Transat before plunging into the world of politics in 1998), insisted he was not taking a page out of the Donald Trump handbook. On the contrary, he claimed that his policies were specifically tailored to Quebec's unique circumstances. Lowering immigration levels would give the Quebec government more resources to help newcomers better integrate into Quebec society, he argued, and a CAQ government would increase the overall investment in French language training for immigrants.

Opposition Liberals didn't buy it. They pointed to an article in *The Economist* which named Legault, alongside Ontario Progressive Conservative Party (PC) party leader Doug Ford and Alberta's United Conservative Party (UCP) leader Jason Kenney,[86] as one of the Canadian political leaders that represented rising populism in Canada:[87]

> In Quebec, nativism has flourished. Its francophone residents have long fought to protect their language and culture. Mr. Legault may not call immigrants rapists—this is Canada, after all—but he does want to cut their inflow by 20 percent, and subject them to a 'values test.'

Legault dismissed the charge and said he would have voted for Hillary Clinton if he were an American. However, shortly after the American election, Legault told reporters that Quebec politicians could glean some lessons from Trump's victory and that he was "comfortable" being compared to the president-elect.

"Mr. Trump was preoccupied by what the citizens wanted," *La Presse* reported Legault saying. "Currently, people are not satisfied with their government; they find that their government is

---

[86] All three men are now premiers of their respective provinces.

[87] "Anti-elitist politicians in Canada are courting immigrants," *The Economist*, April 19, 2018.

far from the people. I think that I'm someone who is close to the people."[88] Polls have shown this to be true—with at least one poll indicating that CAQ popularity rose after the election. The CAQ won a majority government with 37 percent of the vote on election day. Eight months later, that poll showed the party had 46 percent support in voter intentions.[89] The government's popularity appears to have increased since its ban on religious symbols for some public employees and its plan to temporarily decrease immigration.

The CAQ's platform has been hotly contested, but it's far from the immigration policies of Donald Trump or defeated French presidential candidate, Marine Le Pen, who proposed a moratorium on legal immigration.[90] "We don't have a homegrown Donald Trump," said Thierry Giasson, a political science professor at Laval University. However, the CAQ's positions on these issues might be attractive to a certain part of the population, he explained. "They will never say it publicly that they do that to bring in ultra-nationalists or xenophobic or fascist votes to their camp, but these people vote … and they're listening to what the parties are saying," he said, adding that he believes some Quebec politicians play on fear or misunderstanding, or even xenophobia. "I think it's a very dangerous game."

Even more concerning, Giasson said, is the complex nature of how immigration and migration work and the fact that many politicians do not appear to have a strong understanding of the system. "Some politicians are confused about the issue," he said. One

---

[88] Martin Croteau, "François Legault à l'aise d'être comparé à Trump," *La Presse*, November 12, 2016, https://bit.ly/2X3saxc.

[89] Raquel Fletcher, "Poll shows CAQ has gained support since election." *Global News*, June 18, 2019, https://bit.ly/2CCU8X2.

[90] Vincent Michelon, "De l'immigration réduite au moratoire, les propositions changeantes de Marine Le Pen sur l'immigration," *LCI*, April 25, 2017, https://bit.ly/2CxP7PB.

example is the Coalition Avenir Québec's proposal to cut down on all types of immigration by 20 percent. "They realized they couldn't do that because they obviously didn't know their law," Giasson explained, noting that immigration is a federal responsibility as well as a provincial one. The provincial government does not have control over the number of refugees that come into (or leave) the province, nor how many people are accepted through the family reunification program, administered solely by the federal government.

The CAQ then revised its policy to say it will only cut the number of "economic immigrants," something Giasson said "causes confusion in the population." Despite the labour shortage, the CAQ claimed it was necessary to cut down on immigration because too many newcomers were leaving the province. Fewer immigrants, the CAQ argues, will allow for better integration and retention. "I think it's really odd math," Giasson said. "I think the solution is to invest in better integration programs, programs to help immigrants learn French."

Identity and Immigration on the Campaign Trail

"Quebec has arrived at a point where, seen from the outside, it's now become difficult to tell the difference between the positions of the Quebec political parties in matters of identity questions," writes Frédéric Boily in *La Coalition Avenir Québec: Une idéologie à la recherche du pouvoir*. Boily adds that the identity question in Quebec politics has "become an unavoidable theme, thereby supplanting the national debate."

Leading up to the 2018 fall election, the issue of immigration was also largely tied to the identity question; incumbent Premier Philippe Couillard called it the "ballot-box question."[91]

[91] Fletcher, "Immigration the 'ballot box' question in Quebec election."

And François Legault was not the only Quebec politician to have been likened to Donald Trump. In fact, it was starting to become somewhat of a sport for media outlets to run stories with headlines titling various politicians as "the Donald Trump of Quebec." The "volcanic" Liberal Health Minister Gaétan Barrette, as Rémi Nadeau described him in an opinion piece in *Le Journal de Québec*,[92] was compared to the American president for resorting to personal attacks. Quebec MP Maxime Bernier also earned the moniker.[93] PQ leader Jean-François Lisée raised eyebrows when he suggested on Twitter that Quebec build some sort of barrier at the border.

For months, news reports had captured images of asylum seekers crossing the US-Canada border at irregular border crossings, at times risking their lives. By the end of 2018, the Canadian government confirmed that 19,419 asylum seekers had been intercepted by the RCMP, with 95 percent of them passing through Quebec.[94] As many as 400 migrants a day crossed into Quebec, many of them passing through an unofficial border crossing at Roxham Road at the Quebec-New York border.

Lisée tweeted that Quebec should build a fence to prevent asylum seekers from crossing. The PQ leader also called for the federal government to tear up the 2002 Canada-US Safe Third Country agreement, echoing calls from the Canadian Council for Refugees and Amnesty International. The agreement forces refugee claimants to request protection in the first country they enter through land-border crossings, but there is a loophole. Asylum

---

[92] Rémi Nadeau, "Le facteur Barrette," *Le Journal de Québec*, August 8, 2018, https://bit.ly/2q2fJFS.

[93] Carl Meyer, "Bernier explains what he has in common with Trump as he unveils his People's Party of Canada," *Canada's National Observer*, September 14, 2018, https://bit.ly/33G34am.

[94] "Asylum Claims by Year: 2018," Government of Canada, accessed November 11, 2019, https://bit.ly/32BuWLs.

seekers who felt that they would not be granted protection in the US under Donald Trump decided to circumvent the agreement by walking over unguarded sections of the Canada-US border, where they would be arrested and then be allowed to apply for protection in Canada.

When reporters asked who would pay for his fence, the PQ leader joked, "The Mexicans." Lisée later clarified that he wasn't proposing a Trump-like wall: he said it could be a schoolyard fence or just a cedar hedge. However, Quebec Immigration Minister David Heurtel didn't find the PQ leader's suggestion—or his jokes—very funny. He characterized the idea to build a fence as "simplistic" and "off-the-cuff." "You don't solve complex problems by building walls," he said seriously.

By the time the official election campaign kicked off at the end of August 2018, things were not going well for the Liberals. More than 20 MNAs elected in 2014 chose not to seek re-election, including eight cabinet ministers. In his first mandate, Couillard had been forced to boot three Liberal MNAs from caucus amid sexual misconduct allegations and fire one of his cabinet ministers for alleged involvement in a corruption scandal, while yet another cabinet minister quit over unrelated corruption allegations. The premier framed the turnover as an "opportunity for renewal" as opposition parties spoke of regime change. The Liberals had been in office for fifteen years (minus eighteen months in 2012 when the PQ formed a minority government). CAQ leader François Legault presented his party as the most logical middle ground. "His offer to Quebecers ahead of the Oct. 1 election is simple: the CAQ is a federalist, economic-minded alternative to the Liberals and a nationalist, identity-oriented substitute for the

PQ," wrote Giuseppe Valiante for The Canadian Press.[95] Polls had shown the CAQ in the lead for over a year and it looked like it would stay that way.

But just two weeks before voters would head to the polls, Legault would make a blunder that nearly cost him the election. The subject at hand? Immigration, an issue where the CAQ "finds itself on slippery ground," writes Frédéric Boily. Immigration soon became a main debate issue after Day 16 of a 39-day campaign when François Legault unveiled his party's platform: the CAQ leader said his government would force new immigrants to leave the province if they don't learn French within three years (he said the government would offer French training for free). They would also have to pass a values test based on the Quebec Charter of Rights and Freedoms, that would quiz newcomers on gender equality, state secularism, and minority rights, Legault explained.[96] He also said exemptions are possible for seniors or people with learning disabilities. "I want to be human. I don't want to ask them to do something that is impossible," he told reporters.

This platform was dependent on negotiation with the federal government, who controls immigration for refugees and family reunification. The federal government would also have to agree to suspend a selection certificate to so-called "economic immigrants," selected on the basis of the job qualification, who do not pass Quebec's proposed language or values tests because the province does not have the power to expel someone from the country.

Even though it was a major tenet of his platform and a major issue in the campaign, Legault stumbled when asked to explain

---

[95] Guiseppe Valiante (The Canadian Press), "CAQ's Legault offers Quebecers 'middle way' as election campaign begins," *Global News*, August 23, 2018, https://bit.ly/2KdF5Yb.

[96] The Canadian Press, "CAQ Leader François Legault on hot seat over proposed French, values tests for newcomers." *Global News*, September 14, 2018, https://bit.ly/2O5a8GC.

how this would all work, and he appeared to confuse the path to citizenship with the process of becoming a permanent resident. As mentioned, Legault struggled to answer basic questions about the immigration system as well as his own proposals for reform. And, at two press conferences in particular, it showed. When asked how long a permanent resident had to wait before applying for citizenship, Legault replied, "Several months."[97] In actual fact, a permanent resident must live in Canada for three years before applying for citizenship. He or she must also speak English or French and write a citizenship exam.

The next day, Legault said he'd spent the better part of the night reading up on the federal-provincial accord, which he planned to renegotiate with the federal government if elected, in order to grant Quebec more control over its selection of immigrants. However, Parti Québécois Leader Jean-François Lisée said Legault's botched answers should "disqualify" him from being elected. "You're not ready to be premier when you don't know the basics of your main file," he said.[98]

A few days later, the most recent poll showed that support for the CAQ had dropped—it was in a statistical tie with the Liberal Party.[99] And in another blow for Legault, a new study, released in the second half of the campaign, challenged what he had been saying about immigration up until then. The report from the Montreal-based research institute, Institut du Québec, showed

---

[97] Romain Schué, "François Legault peine à expliquer le fonctionnement du système d'immigration," *Radio-Canada*, September 15, 2018, https://bit.ly/36YeB6H.

[98] The Canadian Press, "CAQ leader criticized for incorrectly answering question on immigration." *Global News*, September 16, 2018, https://bit.ly/2X3tuQI.

[99] Guiseppe Valiante (The Canadian Press), "Immigration attacks continue between Quebec party leaders after English debate, *Global News*, September 18, 2018, https://bit.ly/2CBDgjv.

the unemployment rate for Quebec immigrants was dropping dramatically and more of them were staying in the province:

> In 2016, l'Institut du Québec (IdQ) published a report that illustrated the major issue of the integration of immigrants to Quebec. Two years later, the data indicates the situation has changed, notably because of a generalized tightening of the labour market. We estimate that updated data and a clarification of key concepts is needed to nourish the public debate.

While the unemployment rate varied between 10 and 13 percent since 2007 for immigrants aged 25 to 54, this latest studied showed that in 2018 it had dropped to 6 percent. Meanwhile, the rate of retention of immigrants was now 84.3 percent five years after their arrival and 81.8 percent ten years after their arrival, contradicting the number Legault had used thus far during the campaign that over a quarter of newcomers were leaving the province. Quebec still falls behind Ontario, British Columbia, and Alberta, but is now ahead of the Maritimes, Newfoundland and Labrador, Manitoba, and Saskatchewan.

Philippe Couillard accused the CAQ leader of fear-mongering. "Legault doesn't talk about immigrants in a positive light, but these people help Quebec," he said. Was Legault straddling a fine line when it comes to immigration, just as Professor Giasson suggested? Was he trying to garner the nationalist and populist vote? Legault said he feared for the disappearance of French from Quebec and that his grandchildren won't speak the language. "If year after year we accept 50,000 immigrants and most don't speak French, it's a matter of time," he said. "It might take one, two, three generations, but it's a matter of time before we stop speaking French in Montreal and that's not what I want."

There was no doubt that the CAQ was attracting the support of an emerging anti-immigration group known as *La Meute*, which translated means "wolf pack." The first time I had contact with the group was outside of the first leaders' debate. They gave me a copy of their manifesto, which called for a tightening of the border to prevent asylum seekers from crossing irregularly. They told me that most of their views, overall, aligned with the CAQ. They called for electoral reform, a reduction in legal immigration, an immigrant integration program in the regions, the abolition of religious classes in public schools, the "recognition of secularism," and more dignity for seniors, all of which were promises in the CAQ program. They also called for a ban on animal sacrifices for religious reasons.

La Meute's endorsement of his party did not sit well with Legault. He said the group's demands were "on the verge of racism."[100] "We can't stop someone from liking you, but I would rather they didn't like me," Legault is quoted as saying to the Canadian Press during the 2018 election campaign, to which he received stark criticism from the group itself. In spite of Legault's remarks, some commentators still expressed their distaste for the rhetorical connection between the CAQ and La Meute. Sylvain "Maikan" Brouillette wrote on Facebook that,

> If La Meute is on the verge of racism that means that you are too, Mr. Legault. I think it's a shame that you use the same methods as Mr. Couillard. As we all know, he likes to accuse those who don't think like him as racist in order to put an end to the debate. But concerning you, it's worse still: it's those who think like you that you call racists. Ad-

[100] Vicky Fragasso-Marquis (The Canadian Press), "François Legault dit qu'il préférerait que La Meute ne l'aime pas," *Le Soleil*, September 2, 2018, https://bit.ly/2Q9en6J.

mit this strategy is deficient.

Legault's desire to distance himself from the group reflected a sense of anxiety about alt-right groups that were becoming more and more influential in both American and Canadian politics. Barbara Perry, director of the Centre on Hate, Bias, and Extremism at Ontario Tech University, and an expert in this field, estimated that in 2015 more than 100 white supremacist groups existed in Canada.[101] "It's the largest mobilization we've seen in Canada," she said. Perry explained that some of these groups are derived from their European counterparts who found growing support in Canada. The debate around the niqab during the 2015 federal election is one example that might have fueled anti-Muslim and anti-immigrant sentiment in Canada, she said, and "Donald Trump really added fuel to that flame."

La Meute is "generally understood to be the largest active group in Quebec, if not in Canada," she explained. It was particularly visible in Quebec after organizing many large protests. Over forty people were arrested at a rally of far-right protesters and counter protesters in Quebec City in late November 2017. Members of La Meute and Storm Alliance protested outside the National Assembly against the Liberal government's systemic racism consultations, which had already been cancelled the month before when the CAQ and PQ voiced strong opposition, claiming that systemic racism did not exist in Quebec.[102] Quebec City police confirmed that some people rallied with the intention of causing violence and were equipped with disguises and weapons such as batons and slingshots with metal marbles.

---

[101] She is currently conducting a second study where she estimates that number as of 2019 is somewhere between 200 and 300 groups.

[102] Raquel Fletcher, "Opposition calls for Quebec systemic discrimination hearings to be cancelled," *Global News*, September 20, 2017, https://bit.ly/2qDYIBP.

Other protests, organized by far-right groups (and often including counter protesters pushing for more inclusion) took place at the border at Saint-Bernard-de-Lacolle, where there was a temporary village for asylum seekers. Prime Minister Justin Trudeau tried to assure Canadians that everyone who walked across the United States border into Canada would not receive any special treatment and must still go through the usual security checks and immigration evaluations. He condemned the demonstrations organized by what he called a "small minority of racists."[103] Trudeau also didn't hesitate to call out La Meute again in January 2018, at the one year anniversary commemorations for the victims of the mosque shooting. He called the group's members what roughly translates to "dumdums," who walk around with images of dog paws on their clothing.

Legault's Mea Culpa

Everything was riding on the third and final leaders' debate: the CAQ and the Liberals were neck and neck in the polls.[104] Jean-François Lisée's Parti Québécois sat at 20 percent, with the leader's own seat at risk of falling to Manon Massé's Québec Solidaire, who had 16 percent support. Sébastien Dallaire, general manager for Ipsos Quebec said the polls reflected the debate about immigration "with regards to deporting people or not. What really came out of that discussion was maybe the CAQ was not well

[103] The Canadian Press, "Justin Trudeau condemns intolerant, 'racist' rallies, urges trust in immigration system." *Global News*, August 20, 2017, https://bit.ly/34StrtH.

[104] According to an Ipsos poll for Global News/*La Presse*, both the CAQ and the Liberals were sitting at 30 percent support among decided voters one week before election day. See Elysia Bryan-Baynes, "CAQ, Liberals in dead heat: Ipsos poll," *Global News*, September 25, 2018, https://bit.ly/2O6U1bE.

prepared," he said.

The CAQ had lost its lead; it was now looking like a minority government was most probable, and it could go either to the CAQ or the Liberals. Legault knew that the election could be won or lost based on how he handled the topic of immigration during that last debate. "I am not perfect," he said. "Sometimes I make mistakes. But I listen and I change." Then, after responding to a question regarding his questionable immigration policies, Legault fired, "The only people we want to expel are the Liberals!" Political commentators called it a mea culpa, but would it be enough to save him the election?

The evening of election day, Roberval, Philippe Couillard's home riding, was not a jovial place. It seemed Liberal staffers already knew the results before the polling stations even closed. Quebec news networks were not long to call a CAQ government and then, a CAQ majority government. It was a crushing defeat. When the legislature was dissolved in August, the Liberals held 68 of 125 seats; now they held just 32 with only 25 percent of the popular vote, the worst election result in the party's history.[105] Ousted Couillard was the last to arrive and one of the first to leave.

One theory is not so much that the CAQ won, but that the Liberals lost. Couillard campaigned on his economic track record of producing four balanced budgets and the fact that he inherited a Quebec in a precarious financial situation that now had an excellent credit rating. But at times throughout the campaign, Couillard could come off as insensitive, and even arrogant. Lisée accused him during the first leaders' debate of having a "deficit of compassion." Opposition parties repeatedly begrudged the in-

---

[105] David Akin, "Analysis: A historic vote in Quebec for every party, a tougher provincial puzzle for Trudeau," *Global News*, October 2, 2018, https://bit.ly/33H5sNO.

cumbent premier for being didactic, a "*donneur de leçons*," especially when it came to the identity debate and the issue of secularism even though his party's own secularism bill was deemed unconstitutional by the courts and heavily ridiculed across the country. He had been dismissive of corruption allegations plaguing the Liberals for years. At other times, he could appear cold and removed from the everyday person, or Joe Bleau as they say in Quebec. He refused to apologize for steep austerity measures implemented early on in his term that were deeply unpopular. His comment in a last-stretch radio interview when he said that a family could survive on just $75 of groceries a week, was seen by many as being out of touch with reality.

However, a few days after his defeat, when he officially resigned both as leader of the party and MNA, he delivered an emotional and heartfelt speech. It might have been the one-term premier's strongest address to the province throughout the entire election campaign. Premier-elect François Legault had already expressed that he was favourable to using the notwithstanding clause, if necessary, to table a ban on religious symbols for some public employees. Choking back tears, Couillard countered this idea with his own philosophical view on immigration. "Newcomers who will fulfill the many available jobs do not represent a threat to our distinct character in North America. To the contrary—each one of them is essential to our growth. It's our responsibility to help them integrate into our society," Couillard said. "Each word, each gesture counts."[106]

The former premier broke into tears when thanking his wife, Suzanne Pilote, who also cried while she hugged him. He said they would both embrace a slower pace of life and spend their free time with their children and grandchildren. Then, regaining his

---

[106] Jocelyne Richer (The Canadian Press), "Quebec Liberal Leader Philippe Couillard resigns," *Global News*, October 4, 2018, https://bit.ly/2X4NiTF.

composure, he continued,

> I want to finish this declaration by speaking about our liberties. Over the course of our 400-year history we have defended them, sometimes with the ultimate sacrifice. They are contained in the Quebec and Canadian Charters of human rights and freedoms. They are precious and fragile.

Couillard warned that if the National Assembly wanted to preserve its legitimacy, it had the responsibility to protect the rights of minorities. rather than restrict them. "Take great care of them," he said, adding that Quebec should "judge people for what's in their head, not what's on their head."

Bill 9

The 2018 election results revealed a stark dichotomy in the province: a major divide between Montreal and the other regions of Quebec. The CAQ went from second opposition with only 21 seats in the 125-seat National Assembly to a whopping 74 seats (eventually 75 seats after the Roberval by-election), but held only one seat on the island of Montreal. Both the Liberals and PQ had their worst showing since their creations, with the PQ winning only 10 seats (after a recount)[107] and losing official party status (for which 12 seats are needed).[108] The separatist Québec Solidaire also won 10 seats and even managed to steal PQ leader Jean-Francois Lisee's Rosemont riding.

Despite Couillard's eloquent forewarning, the CAQ proceeded with their plan to reform Quebec's immigration system.

[107] They shortly dropped back down to nine seats when Catherine Fournier left the party in March 2019 to sit as an independent.

[108] It later regained party status after negotiating with the other parties.

Simon Jolin-Barrette, the new Immigration Minister, who was a 32-year-old lawyer, tabled legislation, Bill 9, that would immediately put into effect a new immigration system created by the outgoing Liberal party, but which was not yet operational. He referred to it as the "Tinder of Immigration." He explained that it would match applicants with jobs before they even arrived on Canadian soil.

Bill 9 also laid the groundwork to implement French language and values tests, as promised, but what created a more immediate controversy was the government's decision to cancel about 18,000 applications that had already been filed under the old first come, first served system, called the Regular Skilled Worker Program.[109] The Minister said Quebec would reimburse the $1,000 application fee and the applicants could re-apply under the new system. However, many potential candidates had already been waiting years for their applications to be processed—an undetermined number of them were already living and working in Quebec. Not only was it discouraging to have to start the process over, but many of them feared losing their work permits or possible forceful removal from the country. Former Economy Minister Dominique Anglade, now Immigration critic for the Liberals, was incredulous: "We're just going to say, 'Sorry. Too bad, too late, we're doing something different now.' The impact? Very negative."

Several months later, on a weekend in June, the CAQ government passed Bill 9 in the middle of the night due to a closure motion, which allows the government to force a vote on its bill after an all-day (sometimes all-night) debate.[110] It did, however, agree to a compromise to give priority in the new system to the people

---

[109] A court injunction forced the government to continue processing the files until the proposed legislation was passed.

[110] Shakti Langlois-Ortega and Alessia Simona Maratta, "18,000 immigration policies cancelled as Quebec government passes Bill 9," *Global News*, June 16, 2019, https://bit.ly/33BGob2.

already in Quebec. Bill 9 was just one of two controversial pieces of legislation the new CAQ government passed that weekend. The other was its highly-contested secularism bill, which included a ban on religious symbols for people in so-called authority positions. In the next chapter, I look at why the government says this bill will not only end the debate about religious symbols in Quebec, but will also help to stamp out racism in the province—and why opponents say the very opposite is true.

Chapter 7
Bill 21

I was away on vacation, like many of the press tribune journalists, when the crucifix in the National Assembly's Blue Room was taken down from above the speaker's chair. It was early July, and in spite of the debate this small wooden artifact has caused over the past decade, its removal was deliberately unceremonious. Despite multiple requests from members of the press tribune for reporters and photographers, media were not invited to be present at the event.

The Bouchard-Taylor report called for the crucifix to be removed, saying that a religious symbol that hangs prominently in the room where Quebec's laws are passed flies in the face of the idea of secularism. However, since then, successive governments have repeatedly rejected the idea. It is widely, and erroneously, believed to be of great historic and cultural significance. "The crucifix is about 350 years of history in Quebec that none of us are ever going to erase," Premier Jean Charest said on May 22, 2008, the day the Bouchard-Taylor Commission published its report on religious accommodations and state neutrality. On that same day, Charest's Liberal minority government tabled a motion (which passed unanimously) in the National Assembly to leave the crucifix where it was.[111]

It's true that Quebec history is inextricably linked to the Catholic Church, but the crucifix in question is not an historic object. In fact, it was installed in 1982, replacing another one that was hung in the same place in 1936 by then-premier Maurice Duplessis, and the replacement soon went missing.[112] "It's proof that at the time, in 1982, we didn't really care about the crucifix," said Jonathan Livernois, a literature professor at Laval University. Historians suggest Duplessis was inspired by fascist dictators like Italy's Benito Mussolini. When the construction of Quebec's legislature was completed in 1886, "there was no crucifix anywhere in the building," Livernois said.[113]

According to research compiled by the National Assembly library, the 1982 crucifix was created by little known sculptor, Romuald Dion. A *Journal de Montreal* article from October 21 of that same year explains that Dion made the cross by hand out of mahogany and used bronze for the representation of Christ. In 1982, the piece was evaluated to be worth $618. When he first came into power, Premier François Legault pledged to leave the cruci-

[111] Jayme Poisson, "The long fight over a 'secular' Quebec," *Front Burner*, CBC podcast, April 11, 2019.

[112] A single crucifix appeared for the first time on the inventory of heritage objects stored in the National Assembly archives in 2005. However, historians didn't know if it was the 1936 crucifix that hung in the Blue Room or another crucifix that hung in the Red Room, where the Senate sat before its abolishment, and was removed sometime between 1969 and 1976. National Assembly historians were only able to confirm in January 2019 that the crucifix in their collection is indeed the one that Duplessis originally hung in the Blue Room. The crucifix that hung in the Red Room is still missing.

[113] Raquel Fletcher, "National Assembly crucifix representing Quebec 'heritage' only 36 years old," *Global News*, November 6, 2018, https://bit.ly/38rGvZK.

fix in the Blue Room, but in March 2019, when the government tabled its secularism bill, it also proposed a motion to remove the crucifix and put it on display somewhere else in the National Assembly where it could be admired by the public as an historic artefact. The City of Montreal had already announced its plan to take down the crucifix that hung in its council chamber for more than eighty years and move it to a new home in a museum.[114] The CAQ government said this was their way of showing opposition parties they were willing to compromise on the secularism issue. The motion passed unanimously and was met with applause.

Montreal *Gazette* columnist Don Macpherson claims this move was disingenuous.

> The Assembly unanimously voted to have it removed. But that was only after it was shamed into it by Montreal Mayor Valérie Plante's announcement of the removal of the crucifix from the [Montreal] council chamber. And before the government presented the crucifix motion, it ensured it had the opposition's support, so that no party would gain a partisan advantage by opposing it.

Macpherson accused the government of being selectively secular, choosing to embrace religious neutrality only where it suited them. "There has been no movement to, say, remove statues of the Virgin Mary from in front of 'non-denominational' public schools, or change the schools' religious names," he wrote. "Or to remove the 10,000 'Saints,' 2,329 'Saintes,' and 648 'Notre-Dames' still in the place-names commission's name bank .... What

---

[114] Kalina Laframboise, "Crucifix removed from National Assembly's Blue Room after years of debate," *Global News*, July 9, 2019, https://bit.ly/2Q9lDji.

they want is the selective secularism that's been called 'Catho-laicity:' secularism for others, but not for themselves."[115]

In contrast to this view, Robert Calderisi cited Jean-François Lisée, who said that in Quebec, as in other countries in the world, "the majority now wants its own rights respected." Politicians will need to broker peace between progressives who "may see this demand as ignorant and consider a complex multicultural world as the only one imaginable" and populists who "may use public impatience to sow division and try rolling back some minority rights."[116] When introducing his government's secularism legislation, Premier Legault found himself in this very divide.

The Next Step in Nation-Building?

In January 2019, before the National Assembly reconvened for the first time with a CAQ government, the newly-elected Quebec Premier, François Legault invited his MNAs to a two-day caucus retreat in Gatineau. There, he told reporters that his government was ready to table a bill that would ban "public employees in authority positions" from wearing religious symbols. These employees would include judges, prosecutors, police officers, and prison guards as well as teachers. He also said he wouldn't rule out using the notwithstanding clause in order to avoid the bill getting tied up in the courts. Lastly, he claimed that his government would pass the bill with or without reaching a consensus with the other parties at the National Assembly.

"The premier was clear with me. He wants to end the discussion about that subject," said Simon Jolin-Barrette, the Immigration Minister and Government House Leader. Indeed, Legault

[115] Don Macpherson, "Selectively secularizing a land of 10,000 saints," *The Gazette*, Montreal, March 30, 2019, https://bit.ly/2CvVdQy.

[116] Calderisi, *Quebec in a Global Light*, 64.

had appointed him "to put an end to the secularism debate" by drafting legislation based on the Bouchard-Taylor recommendations. But Bill 21 is not Bouchard-Taylor, and both authors of the 2008 report—historian Gérard Bouchard and philosopher Charles Taylor—came out against the legislation. The 2008 report recommended that public sector employees in positions of coercive authority, such as judges, police officers, and prison guards should not be permitted to wear religious symbols on the job, but the CAQ also included public sector teachers, whom they strongly believed were in "authority positions" as well.

"The teachers were not included in our recommendations because we had no proof that it was detrimental to the church, the teaching, or the children. And this is exactly what I'm criticizing in this project today. They have no proof," Bouchard explained during public hearings for Bill 21. The Quebec Federation of School Boards also called for teachers to be excluded from the religious symbols ban, but the CAQ MNA for Iberville, Claire Samson, explained that she was representing her constituents when she supported a religious symbols ban for teachers, even if she herself isn't too preoccupied with it. "They feel that we've taken the religion out of the schools fifty years ago and it's not its place," she said, before explaining that she personally was "raised by nuns" in Catholic school her entire life. "And that didn't make me a more religious person than the guy next door."

After much debate within the caucus itself, Bill 21 also included a grandfather clause in the bill, which would allow employees who currently wear religious symbols to keep their jobs, although they would be barred from any future promotions or transfers. The highly contentious secularism bill also prohibits religious face coverings for all public employees and citizens receiving public services. Legault said that clear secularism legislation would combat extremists and racists in Quebec. "If we say, 'These are the rules. This is the framework,' it will prevent extremists [and] racists [from asking] for the ban of religious signs everywhere in Quebec," he said. [117]

Legault justified his government's bill to Quebecers in a Facebook video he posted once the bill was tabled,. This is a debate that has been ongoing for ten years, he said. There is no conflict between secularism and freedom of religion: Quebecers remain free to practise their religion. Bill 21 is "as moderate as Quebecers," he went on, it respects Quebecers' history and values, and it represents an approach that a great majority of Quebecers want. It's time, he said, to set some rules, "because in Quebec, this is how we live."[118]

But many Quebecers do not think Bill 21 is a moderate bill that reflects "how we live"—lawyers and civil rights advocates argued the bill infringed on charter rights.[119] Benjamin Berger, a professor at Osgoode Hall Law School said, "This is an act that I take to be fundamentally discriminatory in nature and fundamentally one that offends freedom of religion rather than advancing it." Natasha Bakht, an associate law professor at the University of Ottawa, agreed. "When [I] go to get [my] passport ... the fact that [the person who is helping me is] wearing a turban shouldn't have any impact on me filling out my passport application," she said. Moreover, Leila Nasr of the National Council of Canadian Muslims (NCCM) told Global News that the bill was creating fear and fury in the public. "We're getting calls from people who are

---

[117] Raquel Fletcher, "Quebec government to table ban on religious signs, mulls grandfather clause," *Global News*, January 30, 2019, https://bit.ly/36YioRt.

[118] Gloria Henriquez, "'In Quebec, this is how we live:' Premier François Legault reaffirms position on secularism bill," *Global News*, March 31, 2019, https://bit.ly/32BSkIw.

[119] A poll conducted in the spring of 2019 by the Angus Reid Institute found 64 percent of Quebecers supported Bill 21.

reaching out saying, 'What am I supposed to tell my two daughters who are studying education in university right now? Do I tell them they're not allowed to have their dream job?'" Nasr said.

The NCCM, the Canadian Bar Association, and others condemned the CAQ's invoking the notwithstanding clause to keep Bill 21 from being tested in the courts. "I think the fact that the government is using the notwithstanding clause indicates that they know this is a violation of Charter rights and they're trying to prevent that process from even beginning," Nasr said. "The government is putting Quebec on a dangerous path," Gérard Bouchard said. "In that sense, I think this is a radical project."

Prime Minister Justin Trudeau also raised concerns: "It is unthinkable to me that in a free society, we would legitimize discrimination against citizens based on their religion," he said. However, Minister Simon Jolin-Barrette said the notwithstanding clause has been used more than 100 times in Quebec, and the province is within its rights under the Canadian Constitution to use it.[120] It does, however, need to be renewed every five years and Parti Québécois Interim leader Pascal Bérubé said he expects secularism and religious symbols will again be an election issue during the 2022 provincial election. "It's going to be a debate in the next election for sure," he said.

About half of the thirty-six groups who testified during National Assembly public consultations on Bill 21 also don't believe it will end the debate on religious symbols in Quebec. Bouchard warned that this legislation was just the latest saga in an ongoing religious accommodations debate that has hurt Quebec's international reputation. He acknowledged social tensions and said he thought Bill 21 might make things worse. "The relationship be-

[120] Maham Abedi, "Quebec is proposing a religious symbols ban. Law experts say it violates charter rights," *Global News*, March 28, 2019, https://bit.ly/32EJ1re.

tween the majority and minorities is not in good shape," he said.

Charles Taylor, who has distanced himself from the original report, also told the National Assembly that he didn't foresee eleven years ago how his report would stigmatize religious minorities and feed intolerance. "Society is full of Islamophobia," he said.[121]

One morning during question period, Québec Solidaire co-spokesperson Manon Massé made an emotional plea for the government to abandon the bill. She compared the bias against teachers who wear religious symbols to that against members of the LGBTQ2 population in the past. "We gays and lesbians couldn't teach or take care of children because 'we were going to contaminate them with our difference,'" she recalled, using air quotes. "I don't wear a religious symbol ... but I'm different—and that's written on my forehead."[122]

Massé explained that she worked at a summer camp in the 1980s, but her boss feared that parents would pull their kids out of the camp if they knew she was gay. He made her promise not to talk about her sexual orientation. Clapping is prohibited in the National Assembly, but Massé drew applause from MNA's from all parties when she said Bill 21 discriminates against teachers who wear a religious symbol in the same way as she was discriminated against.

However, the Premier stuck to his guns, replying that Quebec's religious signs ban is not that different from what is already in place in Germany, France, and Belgium. "We will not be the only place in the world where some people cannot wear a religious sign," said François Legault. In fact, Calderisi points out in

---

[121] Raquel Fletcher, "Both authors of Bouchard-Taylor report speak out against Quebec's secularism bill," *Global News*, May 8, 2019, https://bit.ly/2rxsuZn.

[122] Question Period, Quebec National Assembly, May 9, 2019.

his book, "Even the European Court of Human Rights, perhaps the greatest bastion of individual liberties on Earth, has justified these bans on the grounds that communal harmony overrides a person's right to religious expression."[123] However, the United Nations voiced concern with several aspects of Bill 21 in particular. [124] In a letter to the Canadian government, UN experts questioned why the bill was necessary. "In particular, it does not establish how the wearing of religious symbols affects the fundamental rights and freedoms of others," they wrote.

They added that the bill did not define what religious symbols were and said they were concerned about potential discrimination. They warned that Bill 21 could be in violation of the International Covenant on Civil and Political Rights and the International Convention on the Elimination of All Forms of Racial Discrimination, which Canada ratified in 1970. "We are particularly concerned with regard to the consequences for those who may be at a disadvantage or excluded from employment in a public position because of the potential effects of the proposed bill," they wrote. But on multiple occasions Minister Simon Jolin-Barrette denied that the proposed law was taking away civil rights. "No, it will give rights to people," Jolin-Barrette earnestly explained to reporters. "It will give rights to all Quebecers to have the right to have secular services from the state."

For many, this secularism bill was the next logical step in nation building. "Bill 21 is the third stage of The Quiet Revolution," wrote Lise Ravary in the Montreal *Gazette*.

> In the 1960s, Quebec Catholic priests and nuns stopped wearing traditional religious garb meant to signify peni-

---

[123] Calderisi, *Quebec in a Global Light*, 53.

[124] Rachel Lau, "UN experts 'concerned,' want answers about Quebec religious symbols bill," *Global News*, May 23, 2019, https://bit.ly/34UZZn4.

> tence and humility, to continue working as teachers or nurses in modernized public education and hospital systems. The second phase was the laicization of Quebec's school system in 1998 when religious school boards were replaced by linguistic ones.

If nuns and priests had to remove their religious garments, she argued that teachers of other faiths should also remove theirs. She continued:

> Bill 21 is a lucid choice made by a mature society after a 10-year-plus debate, a balancing act between individual rights and the legitimate aspirations of a distinct people to choose how they want to live in their historical homeland.[125]

Ravary argued that "full-blown multiculturalism" encourages newcomers to keep their own language and culture and as such, does not promote integration. Similarly, Léolane Kemner wrote in the *Journal de Québec*, "The present chapter on secularism paves the way for all new and brilliant defenders of the Québécois nation, who reveal themselves as indefatigable, devoted, thoughtful and ardent in the protection of our achievements since the Quiet Revolution and our fundamental rights."[126]

Premier Legault said he was "very proud" of his government's secularism bill and believed that history would regard it as one of the most defining pieces of legislation to shape the direction of Quebec society, like the 1977 Charter of the French Language, known as Bill 101. But Pierre Arcand, interim Liberal leader, predicted history would not see the religious symbols bill as a pro-

[125] Lise Ravary, "Bill 21 a lucid choice by a mature society after long debate," *The Gazette*, Montreal, June 25, 2019, https://bit.ly/2KcqEDQ.

[126] Léolane Kemner, "Les livres de demain," *Le Journal de Québec*, May 12, 2019.

gressive piece of legislation: "This botched bill, that can't be applied, that violates the rights of minorities—Mr. Premier, we will remember you for this," he said.[127]

Montreal and Civil Disobedience

Opposition to Bill 21 might not have been entirely concentrated in Montreal, but it was certainly the loudest in Quebec's largest city. Various protests attracted hundreds of people: they made human chains,[128] staged hunger strikes,[129] and spoke of civil disobedience.[130] The City of Montreal declared that the bill violated the Canadian and Quebec Charters of Rights and Freedoms. In a joint declaration, Montreal Mayor Valérie Plante and the opposition party, Ensemble Montréal, protested that the legislation did not "reflect the current daily reality of Montreal society that is rich and unique in terms of culture." Plante said Montreal would be particularly impacted by the legislation because of its diversity, and she was concerned the new law would put that in jeopardy. "Montreal was built thanks to those who chose it as a home. It's what made Montreal a diverse and vibrant city," she said.[131] Lionel Perez, the interim leader of opposition Ensemble Montréal, who also wears a kippa, became emotional during one evening

---

[127] The Canadian Press, "Quebec bans religious symbols for state workers in new law," *Global News*, June 16, 2019, https://bit.ly/2X5CWTz.

[128] Susan Schwartz, "Human chain formed in Old Montreal to protest against Bill 21," *The Gazette*, Montreal, May 7, 2019, https://bit.ly/2KdKbnh.

[129] Phil Carpenter, "Protesters stage hunger strike against Quebec secularism law," *Global News*, June 19, 2019, https://bit.ly/2KdwXXP.

[130] Dan Spector, "Will Montreal defy Quebec's secularism bill?" *Global News*, April 3, 2019, https://bit.ly/2NZYVaB.

[131] Gloria Henriquez, "Montreal Mayor Valérie Plante speaks at Bill 21 parliamentary hearings," *Global News*, May 14, 2019, https://bit.ly/2CzSSUJ.

council meeting. "I'm a Quebecer as much as everyone else," he said to great applause.

Plante, who received threats of physical violence online for her position,[132] also questioned how the proposed law would be enforced. "The application of the law seems hard—impossible, actually," she said. The majority of English Quebecers in particular were vehemently opposed to the legislation. A poll commissioned by the Quebec Community Groups Network (QCGN) found that 60 percent of anglophones believed Bill 21 contravened the Canadian and Quebec Charters of Rights and Freedoms.[133] Both the English Montreal School Board and the Lester B. Pearson School Board passed resolutions that they would not implement Bill 21 if passed. "This proposed legislation would be contrary to the values the EMSB teaches its children, in particular, values of diversity, acceptance, tolerance, and respect for individual rights and religious freedoms," Julien Feldman, chairman of the EMSB's human resources committee said in a statement.

English school organizations collectively spoke out against the bill, testifying at the public consultations that the religious symbols ban contradicts the constitutional right of Quebec's English-speaking minority.[134] Quebec English School Boards Association (QESBA), the Quebec Provincial Association of Teachers, the Association of Directors General of the English School Boards of Quebec, and the English Parents' Committee Association (EPCA) all spoke out against the bill. They claim that article 23 of the Canadian Charter of Rights, which protects minority-language rights and is not subject to the notwithstanding clause, provides

---

[132] Gloria Henriquez, "Montreal Mayor Valérie Plante."

[133] Gloria Henriquez, "Data suggests anglophone support for Bill 21 lower than CAQ says: QCGN," *Global News*, May 23, 2019, https://bit.ly/2X6moLk.

[134] Gloria Henriquez, "Quebec English School Boards Association speaks at Bill 21 hearings," *Global News*, May 14, 2019, https://bit.ly/2KblxUo.

that English school boards have the right to hire who they want, including people with religious symbols. The group explained that on top of that, they hadn't received a single complaint about religious symbols in the past twenty years.

"We've never heard any [issue] on this .... Our students learn from other cultures and other religions," said Sylvain Racette with the Association of Director Generals of English Schools of Quebec. "It is an unnecessary piece of legislation that can only lead to societal discrimination. The government is proposing ... to address a problem that does not exist," said Russell Copeman, QESBA's executive director. He argued further, "I'm the same person whether I wear my kippah or not. I have the same convictions, the same faith, the same principles. I act the same way. How does the kippah on my head change the situation? How does it become a threat in a school to have a teacher wearing a kippah?" He added that banning someone from teaching because he or she wears a religious symbol would only exacerbate the teaching shortage.

A number of Montreal boroughs, particularly those with large anglophone populations, avowed that they would also not comply with the law.[135] "It is unthinkable that we are entertaining removing some rights from very qualified, competent and caring individuals because of their personal faith," said Baie-d'Urfé Mayor Maria Tutino. "I would expect that the majority of the town councilors would vote with me to defy the law." The mayor of Hampstead, William Steinberg, could not contain his disgust with the proposed law. "This is ethnic cleansing—not with a gun but with a law," he said during a press conference. "It's racist. It is despicable."

Steinberg was publicly criticized by politicians from all sides for going too far and he was called on to apologize, even from

[135] Spector, "Will Montreal defy Quebec's secularism bill?"

political allies. Liberal MNA David Birnbaum called Steinberg's comments "hurtful to all Quebecers." "It's not responsible and it's not worthy of his very passionate opposition of which I share to Bill 21," he said.

However, Steinberg dug in: "To apologize would be to say that my arguments were wrong somehow and I'm not going to do that." On more than one occasion, Premier Legault called for calm around this debate, but Bill 21 was no ordinary piece of legislation—it elicited strong reactions, gut reactions: for so many, it was personal and it was offensive.

For Mustafa Farooq, the executive director of the National Council of Canadian Muslims, it went against everything he thought Canada stood for. "I can't help but tear up when I hear the opening swell of the anthem, the swirl of emotions, the feeling of belonging, the promise of a multicultural paradise … I think that's why [the] proposed legislation in Quebec, Bill 21, makes me so profoundly sad," he wrote in the Edmonton Journal in June 2019. "My mother—a junior figure skating champion, a Montessori teacher, [and] one of the most ethical human beings I have ever met—wouldn't be allowed to become a teacher, simply because she wears the hijab," he continued.[136]

Bill 21 is Adopted

Once adopted, criticism of Bill 21 from commentators outside of Quebec was particularly scathing: "They finally fucking did it in Quebec, didn't they?" asked Jesse Brown, indignantly. The host of the Canadaland podcast and former Montreal resident didn't hold back his true feelings about Bill 21 in his July 10, 2019 epi-

[136] Mustafa Farooq, "Opinion: Standing on guard against Quebec's unconstitutional Bill 21," *The Edmonton Journal*, June 8, 2019, https://bit.ly/2Q4yVgS.

sode titled, "F★★k you for this one, Quebec" with co-host Sarah Hagi. "It's always been hovering over Quebec: are they going to ban religious symbols or not and they really did it," Hagi said. "It's a fucking embarrassment. It's humiliating. I mean, just for Canada, that's so embarrassing," Brown replied.

In an interview with Global News radio host, Alex Pierson,[137] Canadian Civil Liberties Association executive director Michael Brown was just as categorical in his criticism of the newly passed Quebec secularism bill. "It's horrible. It's not Canadian. It's not even something that I think would happen in the United States, and that says a lot," he said. "Normally it takes a few years before hubris sets in. They (the CAQ government) went straight to the most discriminatory and horrendous legislation that one could imagine in one of their first bills." Brown called the legislation "Islamaphobic," "racist," and a "blatant violation of people's equality and liberty and freedom." He said that regardless of the notwithstanding clause, the association he represents is prepared to fight the legislation all the way to the Supreme Court.

Despite the reaction to the bill in the national media, the Quebec premier remained unfazed. "As premier of Quebec, it's my responsibility to defend Quebec values in front of the rest of Canada," he told reporters shortly before the bill was adopted. "The vast majority of Quebecers want religious signs to be forbidden for certain groups of employees and that's what I'm doing. People in the rest of Canada, they may be in disagreement with that, but I think that I'm working for Quebecers."

In a marathon National Assembly debate that took all weekend, the Quebec government forced the adoption of its two most contentious bills in mid-June 2019—Bill 9 on immigration and Bill 21 on secularism. On religious symbols, the Parti Québécois

[137] Pierson, "For all the criticism we hear leveled at Donald Trump … who are we to talk?"

voted with the government, while the Liberals and Québec Solidaire were opposed. With the adoption of the bill, the government also adopted several amendments it believed strengthened the bill. First, it defined the parameters of a "religious symbol."[138] And, with the addition of two last-minute amendments, it finally answered the question of how the bill would be enforced. These eleventh-hour amendments allowed for a minister to verify whether the law is being obeyed and to demand "disciplinary measures" as laid out in an employee's collective agreement or employment contract.

"Some organizations say 'We will not apply the bill.' So we need to have the power to verify if the law is enforced," Minister Simon Jolin-Barrette said. He explained that if an organization refuses to apply Bill 21, the government will have the power to seek a court injunction to force it to do so. Opposition parties accused the Minister of acting on the sly. Liberal MNA Marc Tanguay, one of the first to sound the alarm, said, "This potential to have…this type of police, wasn't part of the debate at all." They feared inspectors would be sent to tour schools, courtrooms or police stations, which the Minister denied. He insisted, "It's a progressive bill and we are really proud of that."

---

[138] The legislation defines a religious symbol as "any object, including a garment, a symbol, a jewel, an adornment, an accessory or a headdress" that is worn in connection with a religious belief or is "reasonably considered to refer to religious affiliation."

Chapter 8
Islam, Women, and the Secularism Debate

I had been eyeing a bright red skirt and suit jacket for a good ten minutes. I recognized the colourful material with its elaborate pattern hanging in the clothing booth in the corner of the room as a West African design. I shook my head. It was beautiful, but surely too expensive. My sister and I were seated at a folding table in the middle of a school gymnasium, transformed into the "Francophone Pavilion" for an annual cultural festival in Saskatchewan's capital city, called Mosaic. Each year, Regina's cultural communities sponsor twenty or so "pavilions" which represent countries around the world. Volunteers stamp festival-goers' "passports" before they can enjoy cultural food, drinks, entertainment, and shopping. The Francophone Pavilion, in particular, boasted that it represented all fifty-four nations of the Francophonie.

On this particular afternoon, my sister was devouring her Quebec-style poutine while I sipped a glass of French wine and tried to make out the lyrics of a Franco-Saskatchewan rapper performing on stage. He would be followed by a West African dance troupe and then a jig performance that included some Métis dancers. But the colourful skirt and its sparkling black tulle underlay kept drawing my eye back across the room. I wondered if the vendor would give me a discount if I bought the matching jacket. "I've made up my mind," I said suddenly, which, for the first time since we got there, caused my sister to turn away from her poutine.

As sisters, we're often able to read each other's thoughts. "You're going to buy the skirt, aren't you?" I immediately approached the lady at the clothing booth and inquired about the skirt and jacket ensemble. My hunch about West Africa was right—she was a designer from Côte d'Ivoire who'd recently been featured at Saskatchewan Fashion Week. She let me try the clothes on—both a perfect fit—and we made the transaction, in French.

As a *Francophile*, being *Fransaskois* was as much a part of my identity as it had become for the Ivorian seamstress—and we had that in common. In Saskatchewan, where the French-speaking community is small, if not tiny, anyone who speaks the language at all is welcomed into the community, which has become a pretty multicultural group—people from France, Quebec, French-speaking countries in Africa, like Senegal and Côte d'Ivoire; small francophone communities in Saskatchewan, Manitoba and Alberta are all united in defending and promoting the French language.

When I accepted a new job in Quebec City, I was warned that should I harbour any illusions, I would not be moving to a life-size francophone Pavilion. Still, I wasn't prepared to have "francophone," a badge I wore with pride in my home province, ripped from my identity. My English accent would forever mark me as an anglophone in Quebec. I hadn't necessarily begrudged the fact—English was my mother tongue after all, not to mention that my French was far from perfect. One of my colleagues still likes to joke about the time I asked him to pass me the *menotte* (handcuff) instead of the *manette* (TV remote).

Once, during my first weeks in Quebec, a new friend kindly offered to take me out for supper. He will likely never forget the look on my face when I took my first bite of beef *tartare*, only to discover that it wasn't cooked. He was puzzled—he had told me before we ordered that *tartare* is served raw. I realized too late that I had confused the word *cru* (raw) with *croquant* (crunchy). He laughed; it was an easy enough mistake for an *anglaise* (English girl). I laughed too, but the label stung a little. There was no animosity at all, but even when my French improved, the label stayed. I was English. I would have to face the fact that I was no longer a member of the francophone club. I imagine that many Quebecers who are not native-born Quebecers or native French speakers, those who have learned French, but speak with an accent or belong to a minority culture group, feel the same way. And I imagine for many of them, it's worse now.

"Many, many minorities will feel like they are not Quebecers anymore, that they are not part of the society," said Liberal MNA Hélène David when the CAQ majority government passed its state secularism bill and partial religious symbols ban. She said that minorities will feel excluded from Quebec society and that their rights are no longer protected. "We want everyone to feel proud to be Quebecers. And now we are sending the wrong message," added QS MNA Sol Zanetti. Opposition parties continued to accuse the government of lacking compassion. On the issue of immigration, Québec Solidaire MNA Andrés Fontecilla, an immigrant himself from Chili, pleaded with the Minister in question period to close the debate with a "demonstration of humanity."

The CAQ used pragmatic arguments in favour of its plan to reform the Quebec immigration system, cancelling 18,000 pending applications (estimated to take a year and a half to process) and instead selecting applicants from a new program that matches skills with available jobs. "What we want is for people who come to Quebec to find a job at the height of their qualifications," Legault said. "To welcome is also to integrate." Immigration Minister Simon Jolin-Barrette said that 59 percent of current Quebec immigrants are overqualified for the jobs they have, adding, "For those who have been here for less than five years, the unemployment rate is double what it is for Quebecers born here." But Québec Solidaire co-spokesperson Manon Massé was sick of talking about immigrants as numbers or in terms of statistics only. "In all these debates about the immigration bill, we've talked a lot about files, programs, procedures and statistics .... We have completely forgotten what's hidden behind all that: real people," she said. "These aren't just files that will be destroyed ... these are human lives that will be turned upside down."

Some people have argued that the identity and secularism debate is a false problem. "There were concerns that politicians and the media were encouraging divisiveness in a society that is generally marked by receptivity and respect of cultural difference," writes John S. McCoy.[139] In the same vein, Montreal mayor Valérie Plante, among others, has argued that new legislation isn't necessary because Quebec is already secular. "I fundamentally believe in the strength of our secular institutions and laws. I believe in it so strongly that it is difficult for me to accept this restriction of individual rights and freedoms," she wrote in an editorial in the Montreal *Gazette*.[140]

Gazette columnist Don Macpherson has blamed Québécor newspapers, which he calls "Quebec's own Fox News" for fueling animosity towards immigrants, particularly Muslims. He specifically called out Richard Martineau, who's written approximately 700 columns about Islam, as well as Mathieu Bock-Cote and Denise Bombardier.[141] So, if Quebec politicians and columnists quit

[139] McCoy, *Protecting Multiculturalism*, 96.

[140] "Valérie Plante: Balancing state secularism and individual rights," *The Gazette, Montreal*, May 14, 2019, https://bit.ly/2q4Jgyz.

[141] Don Macpherson, "Opinion: Quebec's own Fox News, only more influential," *The Gazette*, Montreal, May 11, 2019, https://bit.ly/2X5elhL.

talking about it, will it go away? Not necessarily. Immigrants and cultural minorities struggling to be accepted by the larger majority in Quebec might also equally struggle in other provinces in Canada. In a column on the Global News website, Tasha Kheiriddin writes that she suspects Quebecers are not that much different than other Canadians when it comes to how we treat newcomers. "So, while Quebec may take the heat as the most intolerant province in Canada today," she explains, "the rest of the country should take a look in the mirror as well." [142]

At the same time as Quebec passed both its immigration and secularism bills, a national Léger poll revealed 63 percent of respondents think the federal government should limit immigration. "Balancing the number of immigrants with a country's capacity to integrate them is sound policy, but it has to be rooted in facts, not fear," Kheiriddin warned:

> As for curtailing religious expression, it cannot be justified unless there are reasonable grounds to do so. Otherwise, governments are simply appealing to—and reinforcing—xenophobia. In an age when populism and anti-immigrant sentiment is on the ascendancy around the world, that is ground Canada cannot afford to tread.

Why this wariness in Canada towards immigration and newcomers? McCoy, a former University of Alberta political science professor and now current executive director for the Organization for the Prevention of Violence, puts forth another theory in his book, *Protecting Multiculturalism*. During the latter part of the twentieth century, Western states began (re)asserting greater con-

[142] Tasha Kheiriddin. "COMMENTARY: Quebec's harsh new laws may echo sentiments felt elsewhere in Canada." *Global News*. June 17, 2019, https://bit.ly/2PAhWBd.

trol over immigration and integration policy. In the 1990's international economic organizations like the Organization for Economic Co-operation and Development (OECD) began warning of the "growth of foreign populations and the problems posed by the social and economic integration of migrants in the main OECD host countries." Rather than being viewed as an economic and social benefit, immigration and newcomer integration were increasingly described as a challenge, even as a potential social and economic burden. Integration policy began to be seen as an area of public policy that required reform. In this sense, the late twentieth century is a period that saw an important shift in the public narrative over the value of immigrants in the West. However, the events of 9/11 represent a tipping point. [143]

There might also be another reason that, in Quebec specifically, Islam is viewed warily. *Maclean*'s columnist Paul Wells has argued that Quebec's divorce from the Catholic Church in the 1960s has, for better or worse, made Quebecers more skeptical of religion. "The Quiet Revolution in Quebec was specifically a rebellion against religious influence," he writes. "Suspicion of religion in politics is often a progressive impulse in Quebec politics."[144] Quebecers, more so than other Canadians, are particularly wary of political candidates with religious affiliations, especially those who wear visible religious signs. According to the results of an Angus Reid Institute survey published in June 2017 which analyzed the attitudes towards diversity in political leadership among Canadian and American voters, [145] Quebec voters were less likely than other Canadians to support party leaders who were Muslim, Jewish, Sikh, or belonging to an evangelical

[143] McCoy, *Protecting Multiculturalism*, 177.

[144] Paul Wells, "Jagmeet Singh's Quebec Problem," *Maclean's,* July 11, 2017, https://bit.ly/2Q9nrJ5.

[145] "Most in Canada, US say they'd vote for more diverse candidates," *Angus Reid Institute*, June 26, 2017, https://bit.ly/32B8KRt.

Christian denomination (the Angus Reid survey did not ask about Roman Catholic candidates).

Only 36 percent of Quebecers were likely to vote for a man with a religious head-covering, compared to 56 percent of Canadians in total, while only 34 percent of Quebecers were likely to vote for a woman with a religious head-covering, compared to 53 percent of Canadians in total. However, as Wells maintains, this tendency in Quebec is often seen as being progressive rather than Islamophobic. As one person from Quebec's Jewish community said to me once: "[Quebecers] were so fucked over by their own religion, they can't understand how a foreign religion wouldn't be just as dangerous."

The Veil

Djemila Benhabib, an activist and author originally from Algeria, is known for being outspoken. She's also known for getting a reaction. "Women who have an absolutist vision of religion, that is to say, who don't accept removing their veil during work hours and who contest the legitimacy of the state to have common norms, yes, these women are fundamentalists," she said during an exchange at the public hearings on Bill 21.[146] Benhabib is staunchly opposed to the hijab, which she has called an "emblem of fundamentalism" that only serves to promote radical Islam.[147] In her 2009 book, *Ma vie à contre-Coran*, in which she argued that the Bouchard-Taylor recommendations did not go far enough, she writes, "The Islamic veil is more political than religious … it crystallizes symbolically an identity withdrawn into itself that

[146] Geneviève Lajoie, "Laïcité: les femmes qui réfusent de se dévoiler au travail sont intégristes, selon Djemila Benhabib," *Le Journal de Québec*, May 7, 2019, https://bit.ly/36UWVco.

[147] Djemila Benhabib, *Ma vie à contre-Coran: Une femme témoigne sur les islamistes* (Montreal: VLB Éditeur, 2009), 61.

resists all change and all openness to the Other."

Protecting women's rights is another aspect of the secularism debate in Quebec that cannot be overlooked. In particular, the Muslim veil--whether it's the hijab, niqab, burka, or tchador--often enters into the debate one way or another. "The claim for the right to wear the Islamic veil in the West has never made so much noise nor made so much ink flow," Benhabib writes in her book. [148] Even if there is only a small number of Muslim women in Quebec (they represent 1.4 percentage of the population), news outlets have dedicated a lot of space to columnists, activists, and politicians arguing against or for women who wear the veil.[149]

Many Quebec politicians in favour of a religious symbols ban have cited France as a model. However, despite the fact that these societies share a common tongue, they are starkly different when it comes to the prickly issue of the Muslim veil. Emily Laxer in *Unveiling the Nation: The Politics of Secularism in France and Quebec* explains that, "While in France a political consensus has emerged that banning Islamic symbols (particularly the burqa and niqab in public space and the hijab in schools) is critical to the 'Republican contract,' no such political consensus exists in Quebec, where issues of Islamic dress and religious accommodation instead remain highly contested."[150]

During the National Assembly hearings for Bill 21, the veil came up over and over again, and those expressing contradicting

[148] Benhabib, *Ma vie à contre-Coran*, 62.

[149] Supriya Dwivedi, "Commentary: Quebec's attempt at selective secularism—again," *Global News*, August 24, 2017, https://bit.ly/34QpMg0.

[150] Emily Laxer, *Unveiling the Nation: The Politics of Secularism in France and Quebec* (Montreal: McGill-Queen's University Press, 2019), 4.

views on the subject were invited to testify.[151] Similar to Benhabib, Ferid Chikhi, who represented an association of secular North Africans, also associated women who wear the hijab with fundamentalism. "They wear it either because they are activists … or because of ignorance, or because, unfortunately, they were born into political Islam," he said.[152] Former Canadian senator Céline Hervieux-Payette received stern warnings from the committee's president for her presentation at the hearings. Citing a book by Ayaan Hirsi Ali, a Somali-born Dutch-American activist and writer, Hervieux-Payette claimed the hijab leads to female circumcision and forced child marriages.[153] Diane Guilbault, president of the feminist group *Pour les droits des femmes du Québec*, went even further, stating that religion, in general, is sexist. Secularism, she said, would provide another level of protection of women's rights. This view is similar to the position held by the CAQ, at least while they were in opposition. "We are not in Saudi Arabia. We are in Quebec. Burqas and niqabs are accessories that oppress women," Nathalie Roy, then CAQ secularism and immigration critic tweeted in November 2016.

After France banned the burkini swimwear for Muslim women that covers the hair and body up to the neck, wrists, and ankles

---

[151] Some people criticized the government for not inviting enough veiled women to testify (see Alyssia Rubertucci, "Few Muslim women speaking at Bill 21 hearings," *City News Report*, May 10, 2019, video, https://bit.ly/2KcfRts). There are currently no elected Muslims in the National Assembly. Eve Torres, a 44-year-old mother of three, was the first hijabi woman to run for provincial politics. She ran in a Montreal-area riding for Québec Solidaire in the 2018 general election, but was not elected.

[152] Guiseppe Valiante (The Canadian Press), "Bill 21: Quebec's secularism legislation praised, condemned as public hearings get underway," *Global News*, May 7, 2019, https://bit.ly/2NEpnrc.

[153] Raquel Fletcher, "Quebec religious symbols debate becomes personal and emotional," *Global News*, May 9, 2019, https://bit.ly/2X29iyI.

(a decision later overturned by the French courts), Roy called for Quebec to do the same. She later backtracked, saying a ban wouldn't be constitutional in Canada either, but insisted that, "Women are beaten and killed around the world for not wanting to wear those symbols of oppression and submission and that's extremely important." She added, "I think that we have the right to question that without being accused of wanting to hurt anybody."

During Benhabib's testimony, she sat at one end of a long table addressing the transpartisan committee studying the CAQ's religious neutrality bill. There, she found herself literally and figuratively opposed to two Liberal MNAs, themselves also self-proclaimed feminists. Hélène David and Paule Robitaille do not agree with Benhabib on a religious symbols ban. They argued that state secularism has nothing to do with the religious beliefs of individuals, and echoing Prime Minister Justin Trudeau, they said the government should not legislate what women can and cannot wear. "These women have some beliefs, some religious beliefs and that's how they express their faith and I think we should respect them," Robitaille said. "You suspend fundamental rights [only] when there's a fear of imminent danger. Here, there's no imminent danger." Benhabib responded that feminists will never agree on this issue. "These are two camps that unfortunately are irreconcilable," she admitted.

Supporters and opponents of Muslim face veils represent "two very different cultural views," according to Kyle Matthews, the executive director for the Montreal Institute for Genocide and Human Rights Studies at Concordia University. He said that, despite evidence to the contrary, this debate in Quebec is seen as essentially localized, but it's not just divisive in Quebec. It's a global debate, particularly in the Muslim world where the burka and niqab are a relatively recent phenomenon. "They are actually quite contemporary," he said, noting that for a variety of reasons, over the course of the past sixty or seventy years Muslim women began to wear veils and face coverings more often. As some European countries have done, some Muslim-majority countries like Tunisia and Senegal have also recently banned the burka and niqab. "It isn't a racial clash, but a cultural clash based on religion," Matthews explained. "It's not only taking place in the West."

The debate over banning these Muslim face coverings is also being fueled by "a sense that the culture of the majority is being pushed aside," he said. However, the debate about religious symbols seems to have had an adverse effect. Indeed, fears around Islamic terrorism have led to a rise in populism and alt right groups. Matthews said more and more scholars are referring to this move as "reciprocal radicalization:" people being radicalized against Islam. Muslims and Muslim women are not just the subject of an enormous amount of debate, they are also *subject to* negativity and public hostility. *Justice Femme*, a Montreal-based group that offers legal support to women said it received forty reports of incidents against Muslim women in the month following the tabling of Bill 21. In two cases, people attempted to rip the hijab off a woman's head. In another incident, a woman was spat on.

This trend in aggressive behaviour towards women is one of the reasons Charles Taylor denounced his own report on religious accommodations.[154] He confessed that throughout the debate around the PQ's Charter of Values there was a secondary effect of stigmatizing minorities, particularly Muslim women who wear the veil, who experienced hateful remarks and in some cases, even physical assault. He said:

> These gestures are the fruit of a minority of citizens who already feed on the hostility towards immigrants in general,

[154] Taylor, "Opinion: Neutralité de l'état: le temps de la reconciliation."

> or towards Muslims specifically, but who didn't dare show it before. This debate has resulted in diminishing or eliminating their inhibitions, and at the same time, it thickens the clouds of suspicion and fear surrounding newcomers.

Taylor added that Quebec, like many other parts of the world, is facing problems stemming from a growing populism. "The phenomenon isn't at all particular to Quebec," he explains, "we saw similar effects throughout the campaign for Brexit in the United Kingdom and in a manner much more marked throughout Trump's campaign for president."

"We've seen Muslim women face the backlash of this conversation over secularism for the last ten years," Gabrielle Bouchard told the committee during public hearings. The president of the Fédération des femmes du Québec explained why her organization changed its position on a religious symbols ban when they saw what kind of hostility Muslim women faced.[155] "It's a bill that is fundamentally sexist," she said. Other groups pointed out that Bill 21 targets Muslim women who wear the hijab, but not Muslim men who grow beards as a sign of their religion, an argument the Legault government has dismissed. "The bill affects all religions, both men and women, so [...] there is no need to do a gender analysis," said Minister Simon Jolin-Barrette.[156]

For Sondos Lamrhari, the first police studies student to wear the hijab who we met in Chapter Four, the issue of religious symbols, particularly the hijab, is straightforward. In July 2018, she told the Montreal *Gazette*:

---

[155] Guiseppe Valiante (The Canadian Press), "Bill 21 targets Muslim women's rights, says Quebec federation of women," *Global News*, May 16, 2019, https://bit.ly/2QftyeZ.

[156] Caroline Plante (The Canadian Press), "Quebec's religious symbols ban won't affect more women than men: immigration minister," *Global News*, May 15, 2019, https://bit.ly/2O74oMC.

> I think the day we accept the fact that there's not only one single way that liberty can be conceived, I think is the day we'll accept, that yes, there are women who feel free wearing the veil, and there are others who feel free wearing the least amount of clothing possible. As long as women feel free in the way they present their bodies, that's what we need to take into consideration and to highlight.[157]

In the end, wherever your values lie in this debate depends largely on how you already see Quebec society. We're not all talking about the same Quebec.

[157] Sondos Lamrhari, "Why I wear the hijab," YouTube, July 6, 2018, video, https://bit.ly/2X4Q5MI.

Chapter 9
Wanted: A Common National Identity

In June 2018, after a long session at the National Assembly, I went home for two weeks to visit family in Regina, Saskatchewan. Because of a seat sale, I chose to fly back on July 1. As is often the case with WestJet, I had to fly through a bigger city in Western Canada, this time it was Calgary, before flying to Montreal and then making yet a third connection to Quebec City. I landed in the *Capitale-Nationale* just in time to see the Canada Day fireworks from the air—a spectacular "welcome home" after a fifteen-hour journey. What better way to celebrate the national holiday than to fly across the country making various stops along the way?

The experience could not have been more uniquely Canadian and eye-opening if I had planned it. Airports are unique microcosms of cultural collision. Members of Canada's many diverse communities literally stumble into one another in small corridors, cramped seats, and packed lines. On a daily basis, airport staff see names they don't recognize, interact with people who don't speak their language, and try their best to accommodate all sorts of needs. For example, on the flight from Calgary to Montreal, there was an 18-year-old girl who was taking her first flight ever, on her very first time away from home, en route to Trois Riviéres. There was a man in a cowboy hat with a very un-Calgary-like accent struggling with a baby stroller. And two students of Asian descent who'd been selected for SHAD, a prestigious student enrichment program at McGill University.

"I'm going to do my presentation on a story from Chinese culture, but I don't want to say more than that," I overheard the first student from Alberta say to the other. They had only just met in the line to board, but they both confessed to each other how nervous they were that they wouldn't match up to the other students from high schools across Canada. "I don't know for sure what my presentation will be on, but I was thinking of doing it on something my mother always used to say in Korean," said the second student, this one from British Columbia. "I assume the other students will do something a lot deeper."

And there was me, the uprooted girl from Saskatchewan flying with her dog in a kennel on an all-day countrywide excursion back to Quebec City. What a mix. When I landed in Montreal, the multicultural, multiethnic, multilingual passengers dispersed, and I had an annoying six-hour layover. I sighed. At least I would get to take my dog, Mosley, out of his kennel. He'd be happy to eat and relieve himself. My plan was also to take him on a walk outside around the airport's public premises, but Montreal was experiencing a heat wave, and neither I nor my fluffy Samoyed could handle the heat. We decided to stay inside the air-conditioned building and so, for the next four and a half hours we entertained ourselves by people watching. Luckily for us, Mosley loves strangers and attracts a lot of attention, which allowed us to meet people and pass the time.

Some people who were bilingual and didn't know what language I spoke greeted us in both languages, while others opted for one language or the other. Mosley was particularly fond of a lady who shared her French fries with him and of a limousine driver who cooed and offered him his bottle of water. Mosley greeted them in the universal language of a dog's wagging tail, while I, ever the journalist, took note of them all. Nothing surprising about that. I had already started writing this book, and the opening section was about how noticeable diversity can be whenever you find yourself in a large group of people in public, such as when taking public transportation. Airports are one of the most multicultural public spaces you can find.

So why was I surprised? I realized that being a political reporter in the National Assembly the majority of the time, I was living in a bubble, a political bubble. I missed seeing and speaking with everyday people, people like me who were worried about making their connection, excited to see family members waiting for them at the airport, or killing time between flights and delighting in the sight of a puppy. Every time they bent down to pet Mosley, I made a mental note: this is what an everyday Quebecer, or everyday Canadian looks like. And this is how they interact with one another, naturally, intuitively. It was beautiful to watch.

But when they are not forced to mix with other cultures, do everyday Canadians also live in bubbles? Engineering bubbles, perhaps, public service bubbles, office bubbles, high school bubbles, suburban bubbles? Mosley is very good at integrating into any group he finds himself in—but the same can't be said for most of us. We tend to stick to our own bubbles, our own groups. It gave me an idea: what if we are all looking at this identity issue from different angles?

This is the key issue: a Quebecer born and raised in a rural community would have one view of Quebec. His or her view would likely be much different from say, a Quebecer born and raised in Nigeria who now lives in downtown Montreal. Is it realistic to define a Quebec identity that encompasses us all?

Seeming to take a cue from Quebec's minority communities, in October 2017, as the debate around Bill 62 was taking place, the governing Liberals began to organize a province-wide anti-racism forum, only to end up cancelling it several weeks later in the wake of strong backlash from opposition parties. Minister Kathleen Weil was shuffled out of Immigration and into the newly-formed Relations with English-speaking Quebecers portfolio. Incoming Immigration Minister David Heurtel announced the government would replace the forum with two smaller one-day events in Montreal and Quebec City only. Minority communities criticized the largely downsized forum of being too focused on the labour shortage and employer needs when it comes to immigration. They also said it was largely devoid of minority representation.[158]

As my parents can confirm, defining one's culture is an exercise in head-scratching. Ask my family from Saskatchewan, and they will say that my living with a francophone Quebecer means I'm with someone who values having a swimming pool over a garage, an SUV over a truck; someone who values living common-law rather than getting married and whose language does not have a word for "fluffy pancakes" (go figure). Living in Quebec City is different from living in Regina in that here, they treat city ice with salt, rather than sand. My grandmother asked me to translate my mother-in-law's *tourtière* recipe, and when my partner came to visit, she made several meat pies, especially for him, using his own family recipe. Imagine how she was taken aback when he admitted that he actually hates *tourtière*. These might be the cultural differences that for my family, at least, are the most noticeable, but they're hardly the things that define a people.

Most Quebecers agree that, as the only majority francophone society in North America—what Premier Couillard so aptly described as the "minority people in North America … here for 400

[158] Raquel Fletcher, "Quebec forum on diversity lacking ethnic representation," *Global News*, December 5, 2017, https://bit.ly/34LRNoS.

years [and] against all odds, still kicking"—the province needs to protect itself from being taken over by the vast English-speaking culture surrounding it. That's not the same, however, as sheltering itself from any and all external influence. Longstanding cultural minorities, as well as new immigrants, thrive in Quebec and contribute to its great culture. What do they have to say in the debate about nation-building and the future of Quebec?

In 1998, Léon Dion concluded his *La Révolution déroutée* (Diverted Revolution) in much the same way that more than twenty years later I could conclude this book today.

> The Quiet Revolution seems to mark the sudden passage from one societal regime to another, from an historic totality to another ... Since the Quiet Revolution, like in all industrial and urban societies, French Canadians have pinned their identity irrevocably to the conditions of progress and modernity. In many aspects, unfortunately, the winds have abruptly turned for the worse over the last fifteen years or so: an accumulation of disappointments on the political and constitutional plans, ... an economic slump, disenchantment about the quality of education, concerns about the status and future of the French language in the unpredictable future of NAFTA, movement of populations, cultural and economic dependence, (and) technological changes.[159]

Today we could also add fears stemming from an unpredictable Trump presidency, climate crisis, and a new digital and information age. Dion later explains that in a modern and increasingly pluralist society, what's best for the individual and what's best for the common good are often at odds:

---

[159] Léon Dion, *La Révolution déroutée 1960 – 1976,* (Montréal : Les Éditions du Boréal, 1998).

> How can Quebec be conceived as a global society that doesn't exclude anything or anyone, that enchants the imagination, stimulates intellectuals, impregnates all societal classes and the whole of the people, and projects itself in the universal under all forms of collective action? Who/what nourishes … the conscience of a common identity anchored in the origins and fortified by the hope of a favorable destiny?

This is a question that has yet to be answered. Will Quebec ever find an answer to its religious accommodations debate? Is this really something the government can or should legislate? If it does, will exclusion in one form or another always be one of the unfortunate consequences Quebec has to contend with? What if there was another solution?

The Secular Monastery

I gripped the bannister of the staircase abruptly, not expecting to feel so unsteady—it's a normal reaction for almost everyone, our tour guide explained; it is after all, the "crooked staircase." It was built in 1770 and each step has been warped in a different place from the thousands of pairs of feet that have scrambled up and down them over the last several centuries. When the three founding nuns of the *Monastère des Augustines* (Monastery of the Augustinian Sisters) came to Quebec City in the 1600s to open a hospital and care for the sick, they brought with them a large wooden trunk with three separate keyholes. It represented the "spirit of community" they have shared ever since. Cloistered until the 1960's, the Augustinians had no contact with anyone--neither family nor friends outside the convent, other than the patients they cared for--the one exception was a 45-minute visit once a month behind an iron grill. The sisters owned no personal property, and not even their clothing, layers of long gowns and a veil that covered their hair, neck, and forehead, belonged to them.

A small rotating door, not much bigger than a lazy Susan, at the front of the monastery allowed the sisters to communicate with the outside world. People left letters, parcels, and on 1800 occasions, even orphan babies. The sisters received them without ever viewing their senders by turning the door around to the inside. The nuns cared for the infants as they cared for anyone who came through their hospital doors, regardless of language or religion.

Once down in the *voûtes*, or the cave-like basement where the sisters stored food and wine throughout the winter months, our tour guide shows us a cannon found from the Battle of the Plains of Abraham. In one battle, when the cannon fire became too severe, the nuns fled, only to return later to find the British infantry setting up their barracks inside the Monastery. The sisters lived alongside the military for the next twenty-five years.

Today, the exposed brick walls of the basement are painted a peaceful white. There is a sound system fixed to the ceiling, and exercise classes are held there; the Monastery has gained world renown as one of the best health retreats on the planet.[160] Visitors can stay in preserved cells like the nuns, where they are invited to disconnect from their phones and partake in various yoga/relaxation classes. They can also get an aromatherapy massage and enjoy the organic, locally-sourced restaurant. It's an active, living museum—in a way.

That crooked staircase is encased in modern design, leading to a third floor of ultra-modern rooms stacked on top of the authentic cells. The open-space concept lobby, tiled with big slabs of modern black ceramic, encircles the Monastery's historic cha-

---

[160] Raquel Fletcher, "Quebec City monastery recognized internationally for health retreats," *Global News*, July 28, 2016, https://bit.ly/32BHBxY.

pel, which is still used for Mass and prayers twice daily. Catholic artifacts bequeathed to the non-profit organization in that same "spirit of community" from the twelve remaining Augustinian sisters scatter the complex. However, the Monastery's new life as a health retreat is completely secular. Prayer time is offered, but not imposed on visitors. People of all religions are welcome. In its boutique, it sells Christian, Hindu, Buddhist, and non-denominational prayer beads alongside herbal teas with names like "Harmony" and "Serenity." The idea of turning the Monastery into a hotel that promotes health came from the sisters themselves, whose average age is around eighty. By embracing Quebec secularism, they were able to preserve their physical and spiritual legacy.

Before Quebec's Quiet Revolution, which was marked by a change in government from the pro-Church premier Maurice Duplessis to the Liberal Jean Lesage, the Catholic Church ran schools and hospitals across the province. In the 1960's, the provincial government took over, expanding its public service, and separating Church and state. I asked our tour guide: "Were the Augustinian sisters sad at the time to lose control of the hospital they founded?" Perhaps, he answered, but they were also relieved. The province was moving into a new era of modern medicine. There were more than 200 Augustinian nuns in the monastery at the time, and although they were college-trained nurses, they were happy to see healthcare become a major preoccupation for the government, he said.

When our tour ended, I headed out to the courtyard where I found a lawn chair and soaked up the sunshine. I twirled my new prayer beads around my wrist and lay back to meditate. In the background were gentle sounds of the wind, or a sprinkler watering the garden. When I think of Quebec secularism, I go back to that courtyard often in my mind, back to its garden, its warm summer sun, its serenity.

Unfortunately, as I've described in this book, there is nothing serene about the current political debate about secularism.

When I first moved to Quebec City at the beginning of 2016, my father offered to come help me get settled in my first week, and we naturally did a lot of sightseeing. For two prairie-dwellers born in a city founded only in 1905 then flattened by a cyclone in 1912, visiting immaculately-preserved 400-year-old buildings was spellbinding. We spent days walking around and admiring Old Quebec. My father, a non-practising Protestant, said his favourite building was the Notre-Dame Basilica, an amazing cathedral filled with detailed mural and ceiling paintings, intricate gold inlay, and historic wooden pews.

The old city is a UNESCO heritage site specifically for its preservation of these historic and often religious buildings. While the Basilica is still a working church, other buildings have been renovated for new purposes, providing architects with all sorts of creative challenges. The Augustinian monastery is just one example; there's also the Musée de l'Amérique francophone (Museum of Francophone America), situated in a deconsecrated chapel, as is the Maison de la Littérature, a massive public library. Many other similar projects also exist outside the walls of the old city and in communities across Quebec where governments and organizations have made painstaking efforts to transform heritage churches into theatres, fitness centres, dwellings, and even restaurants.[161]

In so doing, they have demonstrated that there is a way to preserve the cultural and religious heritage of the province's founding peoples— First Nations peoples, the first French and English settlers, Irish refugees, and all other cultural minorities that live

[161] Dan Bilefsky, "Where Churches Have Become Temples of Cheese, Fitness and Eroticism," *The New York Times*, July 30, 2018, https://nyti.ms/2XaAb3t.

and flourish in Quebec—and do so in a secular way that benefits the public good. Perhaps the problem is that the current political debate focuses on what to exclude, rather than what to *include* in that common project. Maybe it focuses too much on what fires to ignite, rather than on what fires to put out. And perhaps that debate distracts from the ongoing work, some political and some not, that is taking place to build a better, more secular Quebec.

Conclusion
Making Quebec a University

I can't say if an increase in immigration poses a threat to the French language or culture in Quebec. Likewise, I can't determine if an increase in the number of devout and practicing Muslims poses a threat to Quebec's staunch secularism. I'm not in a position to know whether those fears are real or valid. What I can say is that while many of the arguments I hear are nuanced, maybe even reasonable, some are hostile. And hostility doesn't always need a reason.

Minorities are not the only ones who bear the brunt. As an anglophone from another part of Canada, however, I seem to enjoy a privilege I don't really understand. My French is far from perfect, and yet I'm often told I speak great French and that my accent is cute. People tell me they appreciate that "at least I'm trying."

To help understand the tension between those who embrace a more multicultural society and those who feel a need to protect traditional "Quebec culture and values," I've spent a lot of time thinking about the man best known for easing racial tensions. On a trip to Cape Town about five years ago, I toured Robben Island, where Nelson Mandela was imprisoned for almost two decades. I saw his tiny cell and the quarry where he was forced to break rocks. Stuck in these circumstances and separated from family, most might have called this experience hell, but Mandela had another word for it. He referred to the island prison as a "university." Why? It was there that he and other prisoners discussed politics, learned from one another, and encouraged one another in the fight for racial equality.

For the one-year anniversary of the shooting, the city of Quebec, in partnership with the Quebec City Islamic Cultural Centre, organized four days of commemorations, including a public forum on "*vivre-ensemble.*" At this event, a man stood up and asked panelists how Quebecers could accept a growing visibility of practicing Muslims with the Islamist radicalization that was going on all over the world. The question was deeply unsettling: the six men shot to death in the mosque that night were faithful, law-abiding citizens. None of them had anything to do with terrorism.

But instead of rebuking the man for associating law-abiding members of their faith with radicalized extremists, a number of the Muslim panelists thanked him for opening up an honest discussion. I realized in that moment that we all have our prisons. In Quebec, and in Canada writ large, ignorance and hatred are imprisoning us inside thick, insular walls. We can choose to stay locked in these prisons or, like Mandela, we can turn them into places of higher learning. So, to my reader, I hope you will reflect on what level of intolerance is societally or personally acceptable. With his question, however unpopular, the Quebec man at that forum found a university, as others have found it in the peaceful Augustine monastery. I found mine on the bus on my way to work.

Acknowledgements

I would first like to acknowledge Linda Leith for having a vision for this book and the faith in me to write it. I would also like to thank Karen Macdonald for all her encouragement. To Susan Fletcher and Maya Johnson for multiple read-throughs at various stages and for assuring me what I wrote was fair and accurate. Also to David Akin, Vassy Kapelos, and Neil Bissoondath for your vote of confidence. To Martin, Eve-Sophie, and Ann-Frédérique for being oh so quiet in the house on your summer vacation no less, while I took over our living room to write! And to all the members of the Quebec Parliamentary Press Gallery who have been so generous with their time and resources on a daily basis over the past four years. You are colleagues, you are friends, you have made me a better journalist—and Quebecers are so well served by your work. I am so proud of what you do!

Selected Bibliography

Auger, Michel C. *25 mythes à déboulonner en politique Québécoise*. Montréal : Les Éditions La Presse, 2018.

Benhabib, Djemila. *Ma vie à contre-Coran: Une femme témoigne sur les islamistes*. Montreal : VLB Éditeur, 2009.

Bissoondath, Neil. *Selling Illusions: The Cult of Multiculturalism in Canada*. Penguin Canada, 1994.

Boily, Frédéric. *La Coalition Avenir Québec: Une idéologie à la recherche du pouvoir*. Québec : Presses de l'Université Laval, 2018.

Calderisi, Robert. *Quebec in a Global Light: Reaching for the Common Ground*. Toronto: University of Toronto Press, 2019.

Castonguay, Alec. *Philippe Couillard: la naissance d'un chef*. Rogers, 2014.

Dion, Léon. *La Révolution déroutée 1960 – 1976*. Montréal : Les Éditions du Boréal. 1998.

Laxer, Emily. *Unveiling the Nation: The Politics of Secularism in France and Quebec*. Montreal: McGill-Queen's University Press, 2019.

Legault, François. *Cap sur un Québec gagnant : le projet Saint-Laurent*. Montréal : Les Éditions du Boréal, 1998.

McCoy, John S. *Protecting Multiculturalism: Muslims, Security, and Integration in Canada*. Montreal: McGill-Queen's University Press, 2018.

Ndiaye, Cheik Tidiane and Webster. "Québec, 29 Janvier 2017: Je me souviens," *11 brefs essais contre le racisme pour une lutte systémique*, ed., Christian Nadeau. Montréal : Les éditions Somme toute, 2019.

Traoré, Diahara. *Des musulmanes ouest-africaines au Québec: Entre subversion et conformité*. Montréal: Les Presses de l'Université de Montréal, 2019.

Singles Essays from Linda Leith Publishing

Raquel Fletcher, *Who Belongs in Quebec? Identity Politics in a Changing Society*

Frédérick Lavoie, *For Want of a Fir Tree: Ukraine Undone*. Translated by Donald Winkler.

Martine Delvaux, *Nan Goldin: The Medusa Warrior*. Translated by David Homel

Pascale Navarro, *Women and Power: The Case for Parity*. Translated by David Homel

Wade Rowland, *Saving the CBC: Balancing Profit and Public Service*

Issa J. Boullata, *The Bells of Memory: A Palestinian Boyhood in Jerusalem*

Stephen Henighan, *A Green Reef: The Impact of Climate Change*

Abou Farman, *Clerks of the Passage*

Rick Salutin, *Keeping the Public in Public Education*